PENGUIN TWENTIETH-C̶E̶N̶T̶U̶R̶Y̶ ̶C̶L̶A̶S̶S̶I̶C̶S̶

PENGUIN ENGLISH POETS
GENERAL EDITOR: CHRISTOPHER RICKS

RUDYARD KIPLING: SELECTED POEMS

Rudyard Joseph Kipling was born in Bombay in 1865. His father, John Lockwood Kipling, was the author and illustrator of *Beast and Man in India* and his mother, Alice, was the sister of Lady Burne-Jones. In 1871 Kipling was brought home from India and spent five unhappy years with a foster family in Southsea, an experience he later drew on in *The Light That Failed* (1891). The years he spent at the United Services College, a school for officers' children, are depicted in *Stalky & Co.* (1899), and the character of Beetle is something of a self-portrait. It was during his time at the college that he began writing poetry and *Schoolboy Lyrics* was published privately in 1881. In the following year he started work as a journalist in India and, while there, produced a body of work, stories, sketches and poems – notably *Plain Tales from the Hills* (1888) – that made him an instant literary celebrity when he returned to England in 1889. *Barrack-Room Ballads* (1892) contains some of his most popular pieces, including 'Mandalay', 'Gunga Din' and 'Danny Deever'. In this collection Kipling experimented with form and dialect, notably the cockney accent of the soldier poems, but the influence of hymns, music-hall songs, ballads and public poetry can be found throughout his verse.

In 1892 he married an American, Caroline Balestier, and from 1892 to 1896 they lived in Vermont, where Kipling wrote *The Jungle Book*, published in 1894. In 1901 came *Kim* and in 1902 the *Just So Stories*. Tales of every kind – including historical and science fiction – continued to flow from his pen, but *Kim* is generally thought to be his greatest long work, putting him high among the chroniclers of British expansion.

From 1902 Kipling made his home in Sussex, but he continued to travel widely and caught his first glimpse of warfare in South Africa, where he wrote some excellent reportage on the Boer War. However, many of the views he expressed were rejected by anti-imperialists who accused him of jingoism and love of violence. Though rich and successful, he never again enjoyed the literary esteem of his early years.

With the onset of the Great War, his work became a great deal more sombre. The stories he subsequently wrote, *A Diversity of Creatures* (1917), *Debits and Credits* (1926) and *Limits and Renewals* (1932), are now thought by many to contain some of his finest writing. The death of his only son in 1915 also contributed to a new inwardness of vision. Kipling refused to accept the role of Poet Laureate and other civil honours, but he was the first English writer to be awarded the Nobel Prize, in 1907. He died in 1936 and his autobiographical fragment *Something of Myself* was published the following year.

Peter Keating was reader in English Literature at the University of Edinburgh until 1990 when he retired to become a full-time writer. His publications include *The Working Classes in Victorian Fiction, Into Unknown England, The Haunted Study: A Social History of the English Novel 1875–1914*, which received a Scottish Arts Council Book Award, and *Kipling the Poet*. He has also edited Matthew Arnold's *Selected Prose* and Elizabeth Gaskell's *Cranford/Cousin Phillis*, for Penguin Classics.

Rudyard Kipling
Selected Poems

EDITED BY PETER KEATING

PENGUIN BOOKS

PENGUIN BOOKS

Published by the Penguin Group
Penguin Books Ltd, 27 Wrights Lane, London w8 5TZ, England
Penguin Books USA Inc., 375 Hudson Street, New York, New York 10014, USA
Penguin Books Australia Ltd, Ringwood, Victoria, Australia
Penguin Books Canada Ltd, 10 Alcorn Avenue, Toronto, Ontario, Canada M4V 3B2
Penguin Books (NZ) Ltd, 182–190 Wairau Road, Auckland 10, New Zealand

Penguin Books Ltd, Registered Offices: Harmondsworth, Middlesex, England

First published 1993
10 9 8 7 6 5 4 3 2

Set in 10/11.5pt Monotype Ehrhardt
Typeset by Datix International, Bungay, Suffolk
Printed in England by Clays Ltd, St Ives plc

Contents

Preface

Kipling began writing poetry, or 'verse' as he was always to call it, as a young child. While a schoolboy at the United Services College he contributed poems regularly to the college magazine, which he also edited. In 1881, when he was sixteen years old and still at school, his parents in India arranged, without consulting him, for the publication of a collection of his poems which they called *Schoolboy Lyrics*. The following year he joined his parents in India, taking a job as assistant editor of the *Civil and Military Gazette* in Lahore. During the seven years he spent working for the *Gazette*, and for its sister paper the *Pioneer* in Allahabad, he wrote and published, in addition to his day-by-day journalism, an enormous number of stories and poems. He also collaborated with his family in the publication of two slim volumes – *Echoes* (1884), a collection of verse parodies written with his sister Trix, and *Quartette* (1885), a Christmas annual to which all four members of the family contributed. Some of the poetry written at school and in India Kipling reprinted in later editions of his work, but the greater part of it he left uncollected. It has recently been gathered together and valuably edited by Andrew Rutherford as *Early Verse by Rudyard Kipling 1879–1889* (Oxford, 1986).

The first volume of his own poetry that Kipling himself authorized was *Departmental Ditties* (Lahore, 1886). This was followed, at distinct points in his career, by *Barrack-Room Ballads and Other Verses* (1892), *The Seven Seas* (1896), *The Five Nations* (1903) and *The Years Between* (1919). All five books contained new poems collected together with poems which had already appeared in newspapers and magazines, sometimes many years earlier. Whether new or reprinted, these poems were by no means the whole of his poetic output.

From the beginning of his public career as a writer Kipling experimented with the linking together of poetry and prose. Sometimes this took the simple form of a few lines of poetry serving as an epigraph to a story; at other times, a poem, song, or ballad within a story; or, increasingly, poems which framed and commented on the story. Many of his books which are thought of habitually as volumes of short stories are, in fact, combinations of stories and poems. Very often the story as originally published in a magazine did not carry the poems with it: these were added when the story was collected with others for book publication. In such cases the publication dates of prose and poetry may be quite different, and, unless external evidence is available, the poems' dates of composition difficult to fix. Furthermore, when reprinting these particular poems, Kipling did not include them in his other volumes of poetry but collected them in a separate volume called *Songs from Books* (1913), with many of the poems expanded or re-written.

There were also poems which Kipling did not choose, for one reason or another, to reprint or collect immediately: political satire published in newspapers; a few lines of poetry accompanying travel articles; poems already reprinted without his permission by American 'pirates'; contributions to books by other authors and to various fund-raising organizations; and poems written specifically for clearly defined separate publication, the most important instance of this being the twenty-three poems he contributed to C.R.L. Fletcher's *A History of England* (1911). As editions and selections of his poetry multiplied haphazardly in Britain and America (including a misleadingly titled *Collected Verse of Rudyard Kipling* in 1912), it became clear that a reliable, easily accessible collected edition was badly needed. The result was *Rudyard Kipling's Verse: Inclusive Edition 1885–1918*, published by Hodder & Stoughton in three volumes in 1919, and in a single volume two years later. Far from clarifying the situation, it added to the confusion in ways that have affected Kipling's reputation down to the present day.

It did not much matter that this *Inclusive Edition* was not actually 'inclusive', or that it carried no editorial explanation or guidance: the textual authority of the individual poems was generally reliable, and that seems to have been Kipling's main concern. The problem lies in the way the poems were arranged. It is probable that Kipling intended initially to order the poems chronologically, beginning with *Departmental Ditties*, but soon changed his mind and started to group poems according to subject. Neither policy was followed through: if there was once a consistent editorial policy it is no longer discernible. Early and late poems are placed close together, Boer War poems are linked with First World War poems, and blocks of 'songs' and epigraphs from the prose works are inserted arbitrarily. To give some semblance of order, dates were placed beneath the titles of many of the poems, but these dates may refer to the subject of a particular poem, or its original publication, or its composition, and very often there is no indication which meaning is intended. The *Inclusive Edition* was reprinted in 1927 and 1933, each time with new poems added. In 1940, four years after Kipling's death, yet more poems were included and the title of the volume changed to the *Definitive Edition*. It has been reprinted in that form ever since.

During the final years of his life Kipling revised all his pub- lished works for the *Sussex Edition* (35 vols, 1937–9). The poetry was grouped according to the volumes in which it had been collected originally, with the 'songs from books' expanded and placed in a separate section, and other poems placed under the heading 'Miscellaneous'. Unfortunately the *Sussex* was a limited, expensive publication, and it was the bulky, chaotically organized, one-volume *Definitive Edition* that remained readily available in print. For the reader who, having enjoyed, say, *Barrack-Room Ballads* or the poems in *Puck of Pook's Hill*, wished to read further in Kipling's poetry, the *Definitive Edition* will often have acted as a disincentive. And, because of the special authority the *Definitive* seemed to carry, it tended to affect Kipling's reputation as a poet in other ways as well. By far the most influential volume of the poetry published in the last fifty years has been T.S. Eliot's *A Choice of Kipling's Verse* (1941). The essay on Kipling which prefaced the selection is justly celebrated, but in putting the poems together Eliot followed the order laid down by the *Defini- tive Edition* and in doing so encouraged the misleading view that there is little change or development in Kipling's poetry.

The present edition contains something like a quarter of the poetry that Kipling published in his lifetime. I have selected poems from every phase of Kipling's career, starting with *Depart-*

mental Ditties. I have included none of his juvenilia and none of
the poems written in India which he himself decided not to select
for *Departmental Ditties*: all of these are conveniently available in
Andrew Rutherford's edition *Early Verse*. The poems are arranged
in chronological order, based on the date of their first publication
rather than their date of composition which, as already mentioned,
is often difficult to establish. On the few occasions where I have
felt it sensible slightly to alter the chronology or where there is
doubt about what exactly constitutes a poem's first publication,
details are given in the Notes.

I have used the *Definitive Edition* as my basic text, though I
have also taken into account Kipling's later revisions for the
Sussex. As far as the poems in this selection are concerned, those
revisions were largely a matter of modernizing punctuation and
standardizing certain usages which were always of importance to
Kipling, notably the use and misuse of aspirates and his idiosyn-
cratic addiction to capital letters. Changes such as these have
been incorporated silently in the text. The dates Kipling appended
to poems have often been rendered unnecessary by the chronologi-
cal nature of the present edition, but where I have felt that the
date is, or has become, part of the poem, then it has been
retained. The occasional footnotes, presumably by Kipling, which
have long been familiar to readers of the *Definitive Edition* have
been transferred to the Notes.

Table of Dates

Burma, Singapore, Hong Kong, Japan, and the United States; travel sketches 'From Sea to Sea'. October, arrives in England; lives in London. Meets Wolcott Balestier, American publisher and literary agent, with whom he forms a close friendship.

1890   *Soldiers Three* and other Indian stories published in England.

1891   *The Light That Failed*, *Life's Handicap*. Visits South Africa, Australia, New Zealand, and India for the last time. December, sudden death of Wolcott Balestier.

1892   January, marries Balestier's sister Caroline ('Carrie'); honeymoon tour of America, Canada, Japan. *Barrack-Room Ballads*. *The Naulahka*, which Kipling had written in collaboration with Wolcott Balestier. Moves to Brattleboro, Vermont. December, birth of a daughter, Josephine.

1893   *Many Inventions*.

1894   *The Jungle Book*.

1895   *The Second Jungle Book*.

1896   Birth of second daughter, Elsie. Bitter quarrel with his brother-in-law. The family returns to England; lives for short while in Devon. *The Seven Seas*.

1897   Birth of a son, John. The family moves to Rottingdean, Sussex. *Captains Courageous*.

1898   Visits South Africa; becomes friendly with Cecil Rhodes. Attends naval manoeuvres with the Channel Fleet. *A Fleet in Being*, *The Day's Work*.

1899   January, on a visit to New York Kipling and his two daughters fall seriously ill. Kipling and Elsie recover, Josephine dies. *From Sea to Sea*, *Stalky & Co*.

1900   January to April, in South Africa during the Boer War; helps to establish a paper, *The Friend*, for the troops.

1901   *Kim*.

1902   The family moves to Bateman's, Burwash, Sussex. *Just So Stories*.

1903   *The Five Nations*.

1904   *Traffics and Discoveries*.

1906   *Puck of Pook's Hill*.

1907   Visits Canada, described in newspaper articles 'Letters to the Family'. Awarded Nobel Prize for Literature.

1909   *Actions and Reactions.*

1910   Death of his mother. *Rewards and Fairies.*

1911   Death of his father. *A History of England*, in collaboration with C.R.L. Fletcher.

1913   Visits Egypt, described in magazine articles 'Egypt of the Magicians'. *Songs from Books.*

1915   John Kipling, an officer in the Irish Guards, missing and presumed killed in the Battle of Loos. *France at War, The Fringes of the Fleet.*

1916   *Tales of 'The Trade', Destroyers at Jutland, Sea Warfare.*

1917   Begins work for the Imperial War Graves Commission. *A Diversity of Creatures.*

1919   *The Years Between. Inclusive Edition* of his verse, 1885–1918, published in three volumes.

1920   Visit to French battlefields. *Letters of Travel, Q. Horati Flacci Carminum Librum Quintum*, in collaboration with Charles Graves.

1921   *Inclusive Edition* of his verse published in one volume.

1923   *The Irish Guards in the Great War, Land and Sea Tales for Scouts and Guides.* Rectorial Address at St Andrews University, published as *Independence.*

1924   Marriage of his daughter Elsie to Captain George Bambridge.

1926   *Debits and Credits.*

1927   Visits Brazil, described in newspaper articles 'Brazilian Sketches'.

1928   *A Book of Words*, collection of lectures.

1929   Visits war graves in Egypt and Palestine.

1930   Visits the West Indies. *Thy Servant a Dog.*

1932   *Limits and Renewals.*

1933   *Souvenirs of France.*

1934   *Collected Dog Stories.*

1935   Begins writing his autobiography *Something of Myself*, published posthumously.

1936   18 January, dies at Middlesex Hospital, London.

Further Reading

The place of publication is London, unless otherwise indicated.

Editions

Collected Verse of Rudyard Kipling, 1912.
Rudyard Kipling's Verse: Inclusive Edition 1885–1918, 3 volumes, 1919; 1 volume, 1921, revised 1927 and 1933.
The Sussex Edition of the Complete Works in Prose and Verse of Rudyard Kipling, 35 volumes, 1937–9.
Rudyard Kipling's Verse: Definitive Edition, 1940.
A Choice of Kipling's Verse, ed. T.S. Eliot, 1941.
The Complete Barrack-Room Ballads, ed. Charles Carrington, 1973.
Kipling's Horace, ed. Charles Carrington, 1978.
Early Verse by Rudyard Kipling 1879–1889, ed. Andrew Rutherford, Oxford, 1986.

Letters

Rudyard Kipling to Rider Haggard, ed. Morton Cohen, 1965.
'O Beloved Kids': Rudyard Kipling's Letters to his Children, ed. Elliot L. Gilbert, 1983.
The Letters of Rudyard Kipling 1872–1899, ed. Thomas Pinney, 2 of a projected 4 volumes, 1990.

Biography

Lord Birkenhead, *Rudyard Kipling*, 1978.
Charles Carrington, *Rudyard Kipling*, 1955.
Angus Wilson, *The Strange Ride of Rudyard Kipling*, 1977.

Critical and Other Studies

Kingsley Amis, *Rudyard Kipling and his World*, 1975.

Jacqueline S. Bratton, *The Victorian Popular Ballad*, 1975.

Jacqueline S. Bratton, 'Kipling's Magic Art', *Proceedings of the British Academy*, 1978.

Louis L. Cornell, *Kipling in India*, 1966.

Hugh Cortazzi and George Webb, *Kipling's Japan: Collected Writings*, 1988.

Bonamy Dobrée, *Rudyard Kipling*, 'Writers and Their Work', 1951.

Bonamy Dobrée, *Rudyard Kipling: Realist and Fabulist*, 1967.

Ralph Durand, *Handbook to the Poetry of Rudyard Kipling*, 1914.

Roger Lancelyn Green, *Kipling and the Children*, 1965.

Roger Lancelyn Green (ed.), *Kipling: The Critical Heritage*, 1971.

John Gross (ed.), *Rudyard Kipling: The Man, his Work and his World*, 1972.

R.E. Harbord, *The Reader's Guide to Rudyard Kipling's Work*, 8 volumes, privately printed; Canterbury, Kent, 1961–72 (1 volume, *Verse* I, 1969, is devoted to the poetry).

Peter Keating, *Kipling the Poet*, 1994.

The Kipling Journal, quarterly from 1927.

Ann Parry, *The Poetry of Rudyard Kipling: Rousing the Nation*, Buckingham, 1992.

Thomas Pinney (ed.), *Kipling's India: Uncollected Sketches 1884–88*, 1986.

Andrew Rutherford, 'Some Aspects of Kipling's Verse', *Proceedings of the British Academy*, 1965.

Martin Seymour-Smith, *Rudyard Kipling*, 1989.

M. Van Wyk Smith, *Drummer Hodge: The Poetry of the Anglo-Boer War 1899–1902*, Oxford, 1978.

Ann M. Weygandt, *Kipling's Reading and its Influence on his Poetry*, Philadelphia, 1939.

'We are very slightly changed'

We are very slightly changed
From the semi-apes who ranged
   India's prehistoric clay;
He that drew the longest bow
5 Ran his brother down, you know,
   As we run men down to-day.

'Dowb,' the first of all his race,
Met the Mammoth face to face
   On the lake or in the cave:
10 Stole the steadiest canoe,
Ate the quarry others slew,
   Died – and took the finest grave.

When they scratched the reindeer-bone,
Some one made the sketch his own,
15   Filched it from the artist – then,
Even in those early days,
Won a simple Viceroy's praise
   Through the toil of other men.
Ere they hewed the Sphinx's visage
20 Favouritism governed kissage,
   Even as it does in this age.

Who shall doubt 'the secret hid
Under Cheops' pyramid'
Was that the contractor did

25   Cheops out of several millions?
        Or that Joseph's sudden rise
        To Comptroller of Supplies
        Was a fraud of monstrous size
            On King Pharaoh's swart Civilians?

30   Thus, the artless songs I sing
        Do not deal with anything
            New or never said before.
        As it was in the beginning
        Is to-day official sinning,
35   And shall be for evermore!

The Undertaker's Horse

'To-tschin-shu is condemned to death. How can he drink tea with
the Executioner?'

Japanese proverb

        The eldest son bestrides him,
        And the pretty daughter rides him,
        And I meet him oft o' mornings on the Course;
        And there kindles in my bosom
5   An emotion chill and gruesome
        As I canter past the Undertaker's Horse.

        Neither shies he nor is restive
        But a hideously suggestive
        Trot, professional and placid, he affects;
10   And the cadence of his hoof-beats
        To my mind this grim reproof beats: –
        'Mend your pace, my friend, I'm coming. Who's the next?'

        Ah! stud-bred of ill-omen,
        I have watched the strongest go-men
15   Of pith and might and muscle – at your heels,

Down the plantain-bordered highway,
(Heaven send it ne'er be my way!)
In a lacquered box and jetty upon wheels.

Answer, sombre beast and dreary,
20 Where is Brown, the young, the cheery?
Smith, the pride of all his friends and half the Force?
You were at that last dread *dâk*
We must cover at a walk,
Bring them back to me, O Undertaker's Horse!

25 With your mane unhogged and flowing,
And your curious way of going,
And that businesslike black crimping of your tail,
E'en with Beauty on your back, Sir,
Pacing as a lady's hack, Sir,
30 What wonder when I meet you I turn pale?

It may be you wait your time, Beast,
Till I write my last bad rhyme, Beast –
Quit the sunlight, cut the rhyming, drop the glass –
Follow after with the others,
35 Where some dusky heathen smothers
Us with marigolds in lieu of English grass.

Or, perchance, in years to follow,
I shall watch your plump sides hollow,
See Carnifex (gone lame) become a corse –
40 See old age at last o'erpower you,
And the Station Pack devour you,
I shall chuckle then, O Undertaker's Horse!

But to insult, jibe, and quest, I've
Still the hideously suggestive
45 Trot that hammers out the unrelenting text,
And I hear it hard behind me
In what place soe'er I find me: –
''Sure to catch you soon or later. Who's the next?'

The Story of Uriah

'Now there were two men in one city; the one rich, and the other poor.'

II Samuel 12:1

Jack Barrett went to Quetta
    Because they told him to.
He left his wife at Simla
    On three-fourths his monthly screw.
5   Jack Barrett died at Quetta
    Ere the next month's pay he drew.

Jack Barrett went to Quetta.
    He didn't understand
The reason of his transfer
10   From the pleasant mountain-land.
The season was September,
    And it killed him out of hand.

Jack Barrett went to Quetta
    And there gave up the ghost,
15   Attempting two men's duty
    In that very healthy post;
And Mrs Barrett mourned for him
    Five lively months at most.

Jack Barrett's bones at Quetta
20   Enjoy profound repose;
But I shouldn't be astonished
    If *now* his spirit knows
The reason of his transfer
    From the Himalayan snows.

25   And, when the Last Great Bugle Call
    Adown the Hurnai throbs,
And the last grim joke is entered
    In the big black Book of Jobs,

And Quetta graveyards give again
30   Their victims to the air,
I shouldn't like to be the man
      Who sent Jack Barrett there.

Public Waste

Walpole talks of 'a man and his price' –
      List to a ditty queer –
The sale of a Deputy-Acting-Vice
      Resident-Engineer,
5   *Bought like a bullock, hoof and hide,*
By the Little Tin Gods on the Mountain Side.

By the Laws of the Family Circle 'tis written in letters of
                        brass
That only a Colonel from Chatham can manage the
                        Railways of State,
Because of the gold on his breeks, and the subjects wherein
                        he must pass;
10 Because in all matters that deal not with Railways his
                        knowledge is great.

Now Exeter Battleby Tring had laboured from boyhood to eld
On the Lines of the East and the West, and eke of the
                        North and the South;
Many Lines had he built and surveyed – important the
                        posts which he held;
And the Lords of the Iron Horse were dumb when he
                        opened his mouth.

15 Black as the raven his garb, and his heresies jettier still –
Hinting that Railways required lifetimes of study and
                        knowledge –
Never clanked sword by his side – Vauban he knew not
                        nor drill –
Nor was his name on the list of the men who had passed
                        through the 'College.'

Wherefore the Little Tin Gods harried their little tin souls,
20 Seeing he came not from Chatham, jingled no spurs at his
      heels,
Knowing that, nevertheless, was he first on the Government
      rolls
For the billet of 'Railway Instructor to Little Tin Gods on
      Wheels.'

Letters not seldom they wrote him, 'having the honour to
      state,'
It would be better for all men if he were laid on the shelf.
25 Much would accrue to his bank-book, an he consented to
      wait
Until the Little Tin Gods built him a berth for himself.

'Special, well paid, and exempt from the Law of the Fifty
      and Five,
Even to Ninety and Nine' – these were the terms of the
      pact:
Thus did the Little Tin Gods (long may Their Highnesses
      thrive!)
30 Silence his mouth with rupees, keeping their Circle intact;

Appointing a Colonel from Chatham who managed the
      Bhamo State Line
(The which was one mile and one furlong – a guaranteed
      twenty-inch gauge),
So Exeter Battleby Tring consented his claims to resign,
And died, on four thousand a month, in the ninetieth year
      of his age!

The Plea of the Simla Dancers

Too late, alas! the song
To remedy the wrong –
The rooms are taken from us, swept and garnished for their
      fate,

But these tear-besprinkled pages
5   *Shall attest to future ages*
That we cried against the crime of it – too late, alas! too late!

'What have *we* ever done to bear this grudge?'
    Was there no room save only in Benmore
For docket, *duftar*, and for office-drudge,
10   That you usurp our smoothest dancing floor?
Must Babus do their work on polished teak?
    Are ballrooms fittest for the ink you spill?
Was there no other cheaper house to seek?
    You might have left them all at Strawberry Hill.

15 We never harmed you! Innocent our guise,
    Dainty our shining feet, our voices low;
And we revolved to divers melodies,
    And we were happy but a year ago.
To-night, the moon that watched our lightsome wiles –
20   That beamed upon us through the deodars –
Is wan with gazing on official files,
    And desecrating desks disgust the stars.

Nay! by the memory of tuneful nights –
    Nay! by the witchery of flying feet –
25 Nay! by the glamour of foredone delights –
    By all things merry, musical, and meet –
By wine that sparkled, and by sparkling eyes –
    By wailing waltz – by reckless galop's strain –
By dim verandahs and by soft replies,
30   Give us our ravished ballroom back again!

Or – hearken to the curse we lay on you!
    The ghosts of waltzes shall perplex your brain,
And murmurs of past merriment pursue
    Your 'wildered clerks that they indite in vain;
35 And when you count your poor Provincial millions,
    The only figures that your pen shall frame
Shall be the figures of dear, dear cotillions
    Danced out in tumult long before you came.

Yea! '*See-Saw*' shall upset your estimates,
40   '*Dream Faces*' shall your heavy heads bemuse.
Because your hand, unheeding, desecrates
        Our temple fit for higher, worthier use.
And all the long verandahs, eloquent
        With echoes of a score of Simla years,
45   Shall plague you with unbidden sentiment –
        Babbling of kisses, laughter, love, and tears.

So shall you mazed amid old memories stand,
        So shall you toil, and shall accomplish naught,
And ever in your ears a phantom Band
50   Shall blare away the staid official thought.
Wherefore – and ere this awful curse be spoken,
        Cast out your swarthy sacrilegious train,
And give – ere dancing cease and hearts be broken –
        Give us our ravished ballroom back again!

The Lovers' Litany

Eyes of grey – a sodden quay,
Driving rain and falling tears,
As the steamer puts to sea
In a parting storm of cheers.
5   Sing, for Faith and Hope are high –
        None so true as you and I –
        Sing the Lovers' Litany: –
        '*Love like ours can never die!*'

Eyes of black – a throbbing keel,
10   Milky foam to left and right;
Whispered converse near the wheel
In the brilliant tropic night.
        Cross that rules the Southern Sky,
        Stars that sweep, and turn, and fly,
15   Hear the Lovers' Litany: –
        '*Love like ours can never die!*'

Eyes of brown – a dusty plain
Split and parched with heat of June;
Flying hoof and tightened rein,
20 Hearts that beat the ancient tune.
 Side by side the horses fly,
 Frame we now the old reply
 Of the Lovers' Litany: –
 'Love like ours can never die!'

25 Eyes of blue – the Simla Hills
Silvered with the moonlight hoar;
Pleading of the waltz that thrills,
Dies and echoes round Benmore.
 'Mabel,' 'Officers,' 'Good-bye,'
30   Glamour, wine, and witchery –
 On my soul's sincerity,
 'Love like ours can never die!'

Maidens, of your charity,
Pity my most luckless state.
35 Four times Cupid's debtor I –
Bankrupt in quadruplicate.
 Yet, despite this evil case,
 An a maiden showed me grace,
 Four-and-forty times would I
40   Sing the Lovers' Litany: –
 'Love like ours can never die!'

The Overland Mail

(FOOT-SERVICE TO THE HILLS)

In the Name of the Empress of India, make way,
 O Lords of the Jungle, wherever you roam,
The woods are astir at the close of the day –
 We exiles are waiting for letters from Home.
5 Let the robber retreat – let the tiger turn tail –
In the Name of the Empress, the Overland Mail!

With a jingle of bells as the dusk gathers in,
    He turns to the footpath that heads up the hill –
The bags on his back and a cloth round his chin,
10   And, tucked in his waistbelt, the Post Office bill: –
'Despatched on this date, as received by the rail,
Per runner, two bags of the Overland Mail.'

Is the torrent in spate? He must ford it or swim.
    Has the rain wrecked the road? He must climb by the
        cliff.
15 Does the tempest cry 'Halt'? What are tempests to him?
    The service admits not a 'but' or an 'if.'
While the breath's in his mouth, he must bear without fail,
In the Name of the Empress, the Overland Mail.

From aloe to rose-oak, from rose-oak to fir,
20   From level to upland, from upland to crest,
From rice-field to rock-ridge, from rock-ridge to spur,
    Fly the soft-sandalled feet, strains the brawny, brown
        chest.
From rail to ravine – to the peak from the vale –
Up, up through the night goes the Overland Mail.

25 There's a speck on the hillside, a dot on the road –
    A jingle of bells on the footpath below –
There's a scuffle above in the monkey's abode –
    The world is awake and the clouds are aglow.
For the great Sun himself must attend to the hail: –
30 'In the Name of the Empress, the Overland Mail!'

Christmas in India

Dim dawn behind the tamarisks – the sky is saffron-
        yellow –
    As the women in the village grind the corn,
And the parrots seek the river-side, each calling to his
        fellow

That the Day, the staring Eastern Day, is born.
5   Oh, the white dust on the highway! Oh, the stenches
in the byway!
Oh the clammy fog that hovers over earth!
And at Home they're making merry 'neath the white
and scarlet berry –
What part have India's exiles in their mirth?

Full day behind the tamarisks – the sky is blue and
staring –
10   As the cattle crawl afield beneath the yoke,
And they bear One o'er the field-path, who is past all hope
or caring,
To the ghat below the curling wreaths of smoke.
Call on Rama, going slowly, as ye bear a brother
lowly –
Call on Rama – he may hear, perhaps, your voice!
15   With our hymn-books and our psalters we appeal to
other altars,
And to-day we bid 'good Christian men rejoice!'

High noon behind the tamarisks – the sun is hot above us –
As at Home the Christmas Day is breaking wan.
They will drink our healths at dinner – those who tell us
how they love us,
20   And forget us till another year be gone!
Oh, the toil that knows no breaking! Oh, the
Heimweh, ceaseless, aching!
Oh the black dividing Sea and alien Plain!
Youth was cheap – wherefore we sold it. Gold was
good – we hoped to hold it.
And to-day we know the fulness of our gain.

25   Grey dusk behind the tamarisks – the parrots fly together –
As the Sun is sinking slowly over Home;
And his last ray seems to mock us shackled in a lifelong
tether
That drags us back howe'er so far we roam.

      Hard her service, poor her payment – she in ancient,
          tattered raiment –
30   India, she the grim Stepmother of our kind.
      If a year of life be lent her, if her temple's shrine we
          enter,
      The door is shut – we may not look behind.

    Black night behind the tamarisks – the owls begin their
          chorus –
      As the conches from the temple scream and bray.
35 With the fruitless years behind us and the hopeless years
          before us,
      Let us honour, O my brothers, Christmas Day!
      Call a truce, then, to our labours – let us feast with friends
          and neighbours,
      And be merry as the custom of our caste;
      For, if 'faint and forced the laughter,' and if sadness follow
          after,
40   We are richer by one mocking Christmas past.

'Look, you have cast out Love!'

Look, you have cast out Love! What Gods are these
    You bid me please?
The Three in One, the One in Three? Not so!
    To my own Gods I go.
5 It may be they shall give me greater ease
Than your cold Christ and tangled Trinities.

'A stone's throw out on either hand'

A stone's throw out on either hand
From that well-ordered road we tread,
And all the world is wild and strange:

Churel and ghoul and Djinn and sprite
5   Shall bear us company to-night,
For we have reached the Oldest Land
Wherein the Powers of Darkness range.

The Betrothed

'You must choose between me and your cigar.'
Breach of Promise Case, circa 1885

Open the old cigar-box, get me a Cuba stout,
For things are running crossways, and Maggie and I are
out.

We quarrelled about Havanas – we fought o'er a good
cheroot,
And I know she is exacting, and she says I am a brute.

5   Open the old cigar-box – let me consider a space;
In the soft blue veil of the vapour musing on Maggie's
face.

Maggie is pretty to look at – Maggie's a loving lass,
But the prettiest cheeks must wrinkle, the truest of loves
must pass.

There's peace in a Larranaga, there's calm in a Henry
Clay;
10 But the best cigar in an hour is finished and thrown away –

Thrown away for another as perfect and ripe and brown –
But I could not throw away Maggie for fear o' the talk o'
the town!

Maggie, my wife at fifty – grey and dour and old –
With never another Maggie to purchase for love or gold!

15   And the light of Days that have Been the dark of the Days
               that Are,
      And Love's torch stinking and stale, like the butt of a dead
               cigar —

      The butt of a dead cigar you are bound to keep in your
               pocket —
      With never a new one to light tho' it's charred and black to
               the socket.

      Open the old cigar-box — let me consider a while.
20   Here is a mild Manila — there is a wifely smile.

      Which is the better portion — bondage bought with a ring,
      Or a harem of dusky beauties, fifty tied in a string?

      Counsellors cunning and silent — comforters true and tried,
      And never a one of the fifty to sneer at a rival bride?

25   Thought in the early morning, solace in time of woes,
      Peace in the hush of the twilight, balm ere my eyelids close,

      This will the fifty give me, asking nought in return,
      With only a *Suttee*'s passion — to do their duty and burn.

      This will the fifty give me. When they are spent and dead,
30   Five times other fifties shall be my servants instead.

      The furrows of far-off Java, the isles of the Spanish Main,
      When they hear my harem is empty will send me my
               brides again.

      I will take no heed to their raiment, nor food for their
               mouths withal,
      So long as the gulls are nesting, so long as the showers fall.

35 I will scent 'em with best vanilla, with tea will I temper
            their hides,
    And the Moor and the Mormon shall envy who read of the
            tale of my brides.

    For Maggie has written a letter to give me my choice
            between
    The wee little whimpering Love and the great god Nick o'
            Teen.

    And I have been servant of Love for barely a twelvemonth
            clear,
40 But I have been Priest of Cabanas a matter of seven year;

    And the gloom of my bachelor days is flecked with the
            cheery light
    Of stumps that I burned to Friendship and Pleasure and
            Work and Fight.

    And I turn my eyes to the future that Maggie and I must
            prove,
    But the only light on the marshes is the Will-o'-the-Wisp
            of Love.

45 Will it see me safe through my journey or leave me bogged
            in the mire?
    Since a puff of tobacco can cloud it, shall I follow the fitful
            fire?

    Open the old cigar-box – let me consider anew –
    Old friends, and who is Maggie that I should abandon *you*?

    A million surplus Maggies are willing to bear the yoke;
50 And a woman is only a woman, but a good cigar is a
            Smoke.

    Light me another Cuba – I hold to my first-sworn vows.
    If Maggie will have no rival, I'll have no Maggie for
            Spouse!

The Winners

What is the moral? Who rides may read.
When the night is thick and the tracks are blind
A friend at a pinch is a friend indeed,
But a fool to wait for the laggard behind.
5   Down to Gehenna or up to the Throne,
He travels the fastest who travels alone.

White hands cling to the tightened rein,
Slipping the spur from the booted heel,
Tenderest voices cry 'Turn again!'
10   Red lips tarnish the scabbarded steel.
High hopes faint on a warm hearth-stone –
He travels the fastest who travels alone.

One may fall, but he falls by himself –
Falls by himself with himself to blame.
15   One may attain and to him is pelf,
Loot of the city in Gold or Fame.
Plunder of earth shall be all his own
Who travels the fastest and travels alone.

Wherefore the more ye be holpen and stayed,
20   Stayed by a friend in the hour of toil,
Sing the heretical song I have made –
His be the labour and yours be the spoil.
Win by his aid, and the aid disown –
He travels the fastest who travels alone!

'I have eaten your bread and salt'

I have eaten your bread and salt.
    I have drunk your water and wine.
The deaths ye died I have watched beside,
    And the lives ye led were mine.

5 Was there aught that I did not share
       In vigil or toil or ease, –
One joy or woe that I did not know,
       Dear hearts across the seas?

   I have written the tale of our life
10   For a sheltered people's mirth,
   In jesting guise – but ye are wise,
       And ye know what the jest is worth.

Danny Deever

'What are the bugles blowin' for?' said Files-on-Parade.
'To turn you out, to turn you out,' the Colour-Sergeant
                said.
'What makes you look so white, so white?' said Files-on-
                Parade.
'I'm dreadin' what I've got to watch,' the Colour-Sergeant
                said.
5   For they're hangin' Danny Deever, you can hear the
                Dead March play,
       The Regiment's in 'ollow square – they're hangin' 'im
                to–day;
       They've taken of his buttons off an' cut 'is stripes away,
       An' they're hangin' Danny Deever in the mornin'.

'What makes the rear-rank breathe so 'ard?' said Files-on-
                Parade.
10 'It's bitter cold, it's bitter cold,' the Colour-Sergeant said.
'What makes that front-rank man fall down?' said Files-on-
                Parade.
'A touch o' sun, a touch o' sun,' the Colour-Sergeant said.
       They are hangin' Danny Deever, they are marchin' of
                'im round,
       They 'ave 'alted Danny Deever by 'is coffin on the ground;
15   An' 'e'll swing in 'arf a minute for a sneakin' shootin'
                hound –
       Oh, they're hangin' Danny Deever in the mornin'!

''Is cot was right–'and cot to mine,' said Files–on–Parade.
''E's sleepin' out an' far to–night,' the Colour–Sergeant
      said.
'I've drunk 'is beer a score o' times,' said Files–on Parade.
20 ''E's drinkin' bitter beer alone,' the Colour–Sergeant said.
    They are hangin' Danny Deever, you must mark 'im to
        'is place,
    For 'e shot a comrade sleepin' – you must look 'im in
        the face;
    Nine 'undred of 'is county an' the Regiment's disgrace,
    While they're hangin' Danny Deever in the mornin'.

25 'What's that so black agin the sun?' said Files–on Parade.
'It's Danny fightin' 'ard for life,' the Colour–Sergeant
      said.
'What's that that whimpers over'ead?' said Files–on–Parade.
'It's Danny's soul that's passin' now,' the Colour–Sergeant
      said.
    For they're done with Danny Deever, you can 'ear the
        quick-step play,
30   The Regiment's in column, an' they're marchin' us
        away;
    Ho! the young recruits are shakin', an' they'll want their
        beer to-day,
    After hangin' Danny Deever in the mornin'!

Tommy

I went into a public-'ouse to get a pint o' beer,
The publican 'e up an' sez, 'We serve no red-coats 'ere.'
The girls be'ind the bar they laughed and giggled fit to
      die,
I outs into the street again, an' to myself sez I:
5   Oh, it's Tommy this, an' Tommy that, an' 'Tommy, go
        away';
    But it's 'Thank you, Mister Atkins,' when the band
        begins to play –

The band begins to play, my boys, the band begins to
        play,
  Oh, it's 'Thank you, Mister Atkins,' when the band
        begins to play.

I went into a theatre as sober as could be,
10 They gave a drunk civilian room, but 'adn't none for me;
They sent me to the gallery or round the music-'alls,
But when it comes to fightin', Lord! they'll shove me in
        the stalls!
  For it's Tommy this, an' Tommy that, an' 'Tommy,
        wait outside';
  But it's 'Special train for Atkins' when the trooper's on
        the tide –
15 The troopship's on the tide, my boys, the troopship's on
        the tide,
  Oh, it's 'Special train for Atkins' when the trooper's on
        the tide.

Yes, makin' mock o' uniforms that guard you while you
        sleep
Is cheaper than them uniforms, an' they're starvation
        cheap;
An' hustlin' drunken soldiers when they're goin' large a bit
20 Is five times better business than paradin' in full kit.
  Then it's Tommy this, an' Tommy that, an' 'Tommy,
        'ow's yer soul?'
  But it's 'Thin red line of 'eroes' when the drums begin
        to roll –
  The drums begin to roll, my boys, the drums begin to
        roll,
  Oh, it's 'Thin red line of 'eroes' when the drums begin
        to roll.

25 We aren't no thin red 'eroes, nor we aren't no blackguards
        too,
But single men in barracks, most remarkable like you;
An' if sometimes our conduck isn't all your fancy paints,
Why, single men in barracks don't grow into plaster saints;

While it's Tommy this, an' Tommy that, an' 'Tommy,
     fall be'ind,'
30   But it's 'Please to walk in front, sir,' when there's
     trouble in the wind –
There's trouble in the wind, my boys, there's trouble in
     the wind,
Oh, it's 'Please to walk in front, sir,' when there's
     trouble in the wind.

You talk o' better food for us, an' schools, an' fires, an' all:
We'll wait for extry rations if you treat us rational.
35   Don't mess about the cook-room slops, but prove it to our
     face
The Widow's Uniform is not the soldier-man's disgrace.
    For it's Tommy this, an' Tommy that, an' 'Chuck him
     out, the brute!'
    But it's 'Saviour of 'is country' when the guns begin to
     shoot;
    An' it's Tommy this, an' Tommy that, an' anything you
     please;
40   An' Tommy ain't a bloomin' fool – you bet that Tommy
     sees!

Private Ortheris's Song

My girl she give me the go onest,
    When I was a London lad;
An' I went on the drink for a fortnight,
    An' then I went to the bad.
5   The Queen she give me a shillin'
    To fight for 'er over the seas;
But Guv'ment built me a fever-trap,
    An' Injia give me disease.

(*Chorus*) Ho! don't you 'eed what a girl says,
10   An' don't you go for the beer;

        But I was an ass when I was at grass,
          An' that is why I'm 'ere.

    I fired a shot at a Afghan,
      The beggar 'e fired again,
15 An' I lay on my bed with a 'ole in my 'ed,
      An' missed the next campaign!
    I up with my gun at a Burman
      Who carried a bloomin' *dah*,
    But the cartridge stuck and the bay'nit bruk,
20   An' all I got was the scar.
    (*Chorus*) Ho! don't you aim at a Afghan,
             When you stand on the skyline clear;
          An' don't you go for a Burman
             If none o' your friends is near.

25 I served my time for a Corp'ral,
      An' wetted my stripes with pop,
    For I went on the bend with a intimate friend,
      An' finished the night in the 'shop'.
    I served my time for a Sergeant;
30   The Colonel 'e sez 'No!
The most you'll see is a full C.B.'
      An' . . . very next night 'twas so!

    (*Chorus*) Ho! don't you go for a Corp'ral
            Unless your 'ed is clear;
35   But I was an ass when I was at grass,
            An' that is why I'm 'ere.

    I've tasted the luck o' the Army
      In barrack an' camp an' clink,
    An' I lost my tip through the bloomin' trip
40   Along o' the women an' drink.
    I'm down at the heel o' my service,
      An' when I am laid on the shelf,
My very worst friend from beginning to end
      By the blood of a mouse was myself!

45   (*Chorus*) Ho! don't you 'eed what a girl says,
                      An' don't you go for the beer;
                      But I was an ass when I was at grass,
                      An' that is why I'm 'ere!

Soldier, Soldier

'Soldier, soldier come from the wars,
Why don't you march with my true love?'
'We're fresh from off the ship an' 'e's, maybe, give the slip,
An' you'd best go look for a new love.'

5   New love! True love!
               Best go look for a new love,
               The dead they cannot rise, an' you'd better dry your
                      eyes,
               An' you'd best go look for a new love.

'Soldier, soldier, come from the wars,
10   What did you see o' my true love?'
'I seen 'im serve the Queen in a suit o' rifle-green,
An' you'd best go look for a new love.'

'Soldier, soldier come from the wars,
Did ye see no more o' my true love?'
15   'I seen 'im runnin' by when the shots begun to fly –
But you'd best go look for a new love.'

'Soldier, soldier come from the wars,
Did aught take 'arm to my true love?'
'I couldn't see the fight, for the smoke it lay so white –
20   An' you'd best go look for a new love.'

'Soldier, soldier come from the wars,
I'll up an' tend to my true love!'
''E's lying on the dead with a bullet through 'is 'ead,
An' you'd best go look for a new love.'

25 'Soldier, soldier come from the wars,
   I'll down an' die with my true love!'
   'The pit we dug'll 'ide 'im an' the twenty more beside
       'im –
   An' you'd best go look for a new love.'

   'Soldier, soldier come from the wars,
30 Do you bring no sign from my true love?'
   'I bring a lock of 'air that 'e allus used to wear,
   An' you'd best go look for a new love.'

   'Soldier, soldier come from the wars,
   Oh, then I know it's true I've lost my true love!'
35 'An' I tell you truth again – when you've lost the feel o'
       pain
   You'd best take me for your new love.'

   True love! New love!
   Best take 'im for a new love,
   The dead they cannot rise, so you'd better dry your
      eyes,
40 An' you'd best take 'im for your new love!

The Widow at Windsor

'Ave you 'eard o' the Widow at Windsor
  With a hairy gold crown on 'er 'ead?
She 'as ships on the foam – she 'as millions at 'ome,
  An' she pays us poor beggars in red.
5   (Ow, poor beggars in red!)
There's 'er nick on the cavalry 'orses,
  There's 'er mark on the medical stores –
An' 'er troopers you'll find with a fair wind be'ind
  That takes us to various wars.
10   (Poor beggars! – barbarious wars!)
    Then 'ere's to the Widow at Windsor,
     An' 'ere's to the stores an' the guns,

      The men an' the 'orses what makes up the forces
      O' Missis Victorier's sons.
15   (Poor beggars! Victorier's sons!)

Walk wide o' the Widow at Windsor,
    For 'alf o' Creation she owns:
We 'ave bought 'er the same with the sword an' the flame,
    An' we've salted it down with our bones.
20   (Poor beggars! – it's blue with our bones!)
Hands off o' the sons o' the Widow,
    Hands off o' the goods in 'er shop,
For the Kings must come down an' the Emperors frown
    When the Widow at Windsor says 'Stop!'
25   (Poor beggars! – we're sent to say 'Stop!')
      Then 'ere's to the Lodge o' the Widow,
        From the Pole to the Tropics it runs –
        To the Lodge that we tile with the rank an' the
          file,
        An' open in form with the guns.
30   (Poor beggars! – it's always they guns!)

We 'ave 'eard o' the Widow at Windsor,
    It's safest to leave 'er alone:
For 'er sentries we stand by the sea an' the land
    Wherever the bugles are blown.
35   (Poor beggars! – an' don't we get blown!)
Take 'old o' the Wings o' the Mornin',
    An' flop round the earth till you're dead;
But you won't get away from the tune that they play
    To the bloomin' old rag over'ead.
40   (Poor beggars! – it's 'ot over'ead!)
      Then 'ere's to the Sons o' the Widow,
        Wherever, 'owever they roam.
      'Ere's all they desire, an' if they require,
        A speedy return to their 'ome.
45   (Poor beggars! – they'll never see 'ome!)

Gunga Din

You may talk o' gin and beer
When you're quartered safe out 'ere,
An' you're sent to penny-fights an' Aldershot it;
But when it comes to slaughter
5   You will do your work on water,
An' you'll lick the bloomin' boots of 'im that's got it.
Now in Injia's sunny clime,
Where I used to spend my time
A-servin' of 'Er Majesty the Queen,
10 Of all them blackfaced crew
The finest man I knew
Was our regimental *bhisti*, Gunga Din.
        'E was 'Din! Din! Din!
    You limpin' lump o' brick-dust, Gunga Din!
15   Hi! Slippy *hitherao*!
            Water, get it! *Panee lao*,
        You squidgy-nosed old idol, Gunga Din.'

The uniform 'e wore
Was nothin' much before,
20 An' rather less than 'arf o' that be'ind,
For a piece o' twisty rag
An' a goatskin water-bag
Was all the field-equipment 'e could find.
When the sweatin' troop-train lay
25 In a sidin' through the day,
Where the 'eat would make your bloomin' eyebrows crawl,
We shouted '*Harry By!*'
Till our throats were bricky-dry,
Then we wopped 'im 'cause 'e couldn't serve us all.
30   It was 'Din! Din! Din!
    You 'eathen, where the mischief 'ave you been?
        You put some *juldee* in it
        Or I'll *marrow* you this minute
    If you don't fill up my helmet, Gunga Din!'

35 'E would dot an' carry one
Till the longest day was done;
An' 'e didn't seem to know the use o' fear.
If we charged or broke or cut,
You could bet your bloomin' nut,
40 'E'd be waitin' fifty paces right flank rear.
With 'is mussick on 'is back,
'E would skip with our attack,
An' watch us till the bugles made 'Retire,'
An' for all 'is dirty 'ide
45 'E was white, clear white, inside
When 'e went to tend the wounded under fire!
        It was 'Din! Din! Din!'
    With the bullets kickin' dust-spots on the green.
        When the cartridges ran out,
50   You could hear the front-ranks shout,
    'Hi! ammunition-mules an' Gunga Din!'

I shan't forgit the night
When I dropped be'ind the fight
With a bullet where my belt-plate should 'a' been.
55 I was chokin' mad with thirst,
An' the man that spied me first
Was our good old grinnin', gruntin' Gunga Din.
'E lifted up my 'ead,
An' 'e plugged me where I bled,
60 An' 'e guv me 'arf-a-pint o' water green.
It was crawlin' an' it stunk,
But of all the drinks I've drunk,
I'm gratefullest to one from Gunga Din.
        It was 'Din! Din! Din!
65   'Ere's a beggar with a bullet through 'is spleen;
        'E's chawin' up the ground,
            An' 'e's kickin' all around:
    For Gawd's sake git the water, Gunga Din!'

'E carried me away
70 To where a dooli lay,
An' a bullet come an' drilled the beggar clean.

'E put me safe inside,
An' just before 'e died,
'I 'ope you liked your drink,' sez Gunga Din.
75 So I'll meet 'im later on
At the place where 'e is gone
Where it's always double drills an' no canteen.
'E'll be squattin' on the coals
Givin' drink to poor damned souls,
80 An' I'll get a swig in hell from Gunga Din!
        Yes, Din! Din! Din!
    You Lazarushian-leather Gunga Din!
        Though I've belted you and flayed you,
        By the livin' Gawd that made you,
85   You're a better man than I am, Gunga Din!

Mandalay

By the old Moulmein Pagoda, lookin' eastward to the sea,
There's a Burma girl a-settin', an' I know she thinks o' me;
For the wind is in the palm-trees, an' the temple-bells they
            say:
'Come you back, you British soldier; come you back to
            Mandalay!'
5   Come you back to Mandalay,
        Where the old Flotilla lay:
    Can't you 'ear their paddles chunkin' from Rangoon to
            Mandalay?
        On the road to Mandalay,
        Where the flyin'-fishes play,
10   An' the dawn comes up like thunder outer China 'crost
            the Bay!

'Er petticoat was yaller an' 'er little cap was green,
An' 'er name was Supi-yaw-lat – jes' the same as Theebaw's
            Queen,
An' I seed her first a-smokin' of a whackin' white cheroot,
An' a-wastin' Christian kisses on an 'eathen idol's foot:

15   Bloomin' idol made o' mud –
      Wot they called the Great Gawd Budd –
      Plucky lot she cared for idols when I kissed 'er where
            she stud!
      On the road to Mandalay . . .

      When the mist was on the rice-fields an' the sun was
            droppin' slow,
20   She'd git 'er little banjo an' she'd sing '*Kulla-lo-lo!*'
      With 'er arm upon my shoulder an' 'er cheek agin my
            cheek
      We useter watch the steamers an' the *hathis* pilin' teak.
            Elephints a-pilin' teak
            In the sludgy, squdgy creek,
25   Where the silence 'ung that 'eavy you was 'arf afraid to
            speak!
      On the road to Mandalay . . .

      But that's all shove be'ind me – long ago an' fur away,
      An' there ain't no 'buses runnin' from the Bank to
            Mandalay;
      An' I'm learnin' 'ere in London what the ten-year soldier
            tells:
30   'If you've 'eard the East a-callin', you won't never 'eed
            naught else.'
            No! you won't 'eed nothin' else
            But them spicy garlic smells,
      An' the sunshine an' the palm-trees an' the tinkly temple
            bells;
      On the road to Mandalay . . .

35   I am sick o' wastin' leather on these gritty pavin'-stones,
      An' the blasted English drizzle wakes the fever in my
            bones;
      Tho' I walks with fifty 'ousemaids outer Chelsea to the
            Strand,
      An' they talks a lot o' lovin', but wot do they understand?
            Beefy face an' grubby 'and –
40   Law! wot do they understand?

I've a neater, sweeter maiden in a cleaner, greener land!
On the road to Mandalay . . .

Ship me somewheres east of Suez, where the best is like
        the worst,
Where there aren't no Ten Commandments an' a man can
        raise a thirst;
45   For the temple-bells are callin', an' it's there that I would
        be –
By the old Moulmein Pagoda, looking lazy at the sea;
   On the road to Mandalay,
   Where the old Flotilla lay,
   With our sick beneath the awnings when we went to
      Mandalay!
50   Oh, the road to Mandalay,
   Where the flyin'-fishes play,
   An' the dawn comes up like thunder outer China 'crost
      the Bay!

The Young British Soldier

When the 'arf-made recruity goes out to the East
'E acts like a babe an' 'e drinks like a beast,
An' 'e wonders because 'e is frequent deceased
   Ere 'e's fit for to serve as a soldier.
5   Serve, serve, serve as a soldier,
      Serve, serve, serve as a soldier,
      Serve, serve, serve as a soldier,
      So-oldier *of* the Queen!

Now all you recruities what's drafted to-day,
10 You shut up your rag-box an' 'ark to my lay,
An' I'll sing you a soldier as far as I may:
   A soldier what's fit for a soldier.
      Fit, fit, fit for a soldier . . .

First mind you steer clear o' the grog-sellers' huts,
15 For they sell you Fixed Bay'nets that rots out your guts –

Ay, drink that 'ud eat the live steel from your butts –
　　An' it's bad for the young British soldier.
　　　　Bad, bad, bad, for the soldier . . .

When the cholera comes – as it will past a doubt –
20　Keep out of the wet an' don't go on the shout,
For the sickness gets in as the liquor dies out,
　　An' it crumples the young British soldier.
　　　　Crum-, crum-, crumples the soldier . . .

But the worst o' your foes is the sun over'ead:
25　You *must* wear your 'elmet for all that is said:
If 'e finds you uncovered 'e'll knock you down dead,
　　An' you'll die like a fool of a soldier.
　　　　Fool, fool, fool of a soldier . . .

If you're cast for fatigue by a Sergeant unkind,
30　Don't grouse like a woman nor crack on nor blind;
Be handy an' civil, an' then you will find
　　That it's beer for the young British soldier.
　　　　Beer, beer, beer for the soldier . . .

Now, if you must marry, take care she is old –
35　A Troop-Sergeant's widow's the nicest I'm told,
For beauty won't help if your rations is cold,
　　Nor love ain't enough for a soldier.
　　　　'Nough, 'nough, 'nough for a soldier . . .

If the wife should go wrong with a comrade, be loth
40　To shoot when you catch 'em – you'll swing, on my oath! –
Make 'im take 'er an' keep 'er: that's Hell for them both,
　　An' you're shut o' the curse of a soldier.
　　　　Curse, curse, curse of a soldier . . .

When first under fire an' you're wishful to duck,
45　Don't look nor take 'eed at the man that is struck.
Be thankful you're livin', and trust to your luck
　　An' march to your front like a soldier.
　　　　Front, front, front like a soldier . . .

When 'arf of your bullets fly wide in the ditch,
50 Don't call your Martini a cross-eyed old bitch;
She's as human as you are – you treat her as sich,
    An' she'll fight for the young British soldier.
        Fight, fight, fight for the soldier . . .

When, shakin' their bustles like ladies so fine,
55 The guns o' the enemy wheel into line,
Shoot low at the limbers an' don't mind the shine,
    For noise never startles the soldier.
        Start-, start-, startles the soldier . . .

If your Officer's dead and the Sergeants look white.
60 Remember it's ruin to run from a fight:
So take open order, lie down, an' sit tight,
    An' wait for supports like a soldier.
        Wait, wait, wait like a soldier . . .

When you're wounded an' left on Afghanistan's plains,
65 An' the women come out to cut up what remains,
Jest roll to your rifle an' blow out your brains
    An' go to your Gawd like a soldier.
        Go, go, go like a soldier,
        Go, go, go like a soldier,
70   Go, go, go like a soldier,
        So–oldier *of* the Queen!

The Conundrum of the Workshops

When the flush of a new-born sun fell first on Eden's
        green and gold,
Our father Adam sat under the Tree and scratched with a
        stick in the mould;
And the first rude sketch that the world had seen was joy
        to his mighty heart,
Till the Devil whispered behind the leaves, 'It's pretty, but
        is it Art?'

5   Wherefore he called to his wife, and fled to fashion his
        work anew –
    The first of his race who cared a fig for the first, most
        dread review;
    And he left his lore to the use of his sons – and that was a
        glorious gain
    When the Devil chuckled, 'Is it Art?' in the ear of the
        branded Cain.

    They builded a tower to shiver the sky and wrench the
        stars apart,
10 Till the Devil grunted behind the bricks: 'It's striking, but
        is it Art?'
    The stone was dropped at the quarry-side and the idle
        derrick swung,
    While each man talked of the aims of Art, and each in an
        alien tongue.

    They fought and they talked in the North and the South;
        they talked and they fought in the West,
    Till the waters rose on the pitiful land, and the poor Red
        Clay had rest –
15 Had rest till that dank blank-canvas dawn when the Dove
        was preened to start,
    And the Devil bubbled below the keel: 'It's human, but is
        it Art?'

    The tale is as old as the Eden Tree – and new as the new-
        cut tooth –
    For each man knows ere his lip-thatch grows he is master
        of Art and Truth;
    And each man hears as the twilight nears, to the beat of his
        dying heart,
20 The Devil drum on the darkened pane: 'You did it, but
        was it Art?'

    We have learned to whittle the Eden Tree to the shape of a
        surplice-peg,
    We have learned to bottle our parents twain in the yelk of
        an addled egg,

We know that the tail must wag the dog, for the horse is
      drawn by the cart;
But the Devil whoops, as he whooped of old: 'It's clever,
      but is it Art?'

25 When the flicker of London sun falls faint on the Club-
      room's green and gold,
The sons of Adam sit them down and scratch with their
      pens in the mould –
They scratch with their pens in the mould of their graves,
      and the ink and the anguish start,
For the Devil mutters behind the leaves: 'It's pretty, but is
      it Art?'

Now, if we could win to the Eden Tree where the Four
      Great Rivers flow,
30 And the Wreath of Eve is red on the turf as she left it long
      ago,
And if we could come when the sentry slept and softly
      scurry through,
By the favour of God we might know as much – as our
      father Adam knew!

'Ford o' Kabul River'

Kabul town's by Kabul river –
  Blow the bugle, draw the sword –
There I lef' my mate for ever,
  Wet an' drippin' by the ford.
5   Ford, ford, ford o' Kabul river,
        Ford o' Kabul river in the dark!
        There's the river up and brimmin', an' there's 'arf a
          squadron swimmin'
        'Cross the ford o' Kabul river in the dark.

Kabul town's a blasted place –
10   Blow the bugle, draw the sword –
'Strewth, I shan't forget 'is face
    Wet an' drippin' by the ford!
       Ford, ford, ford o' Kabul river,
        Ford o' Kabul river in the dark!
15   Keep the crossing-stakes beside you, an' they will
          surely guide you
       'Cross the ford o' Kabul river in the dark.

Kabul town is sun an' dust –
    Blow the bugle, draw the sword –
I'd ha' sooner drownded fust
20   'Stead of 'im beside the ford.
       Ford, ford, ford o' Kabul river,
        Ford o' Kabul river in the dark!
       You can 'ear the 'orses threshin'; you can 'ear the
          men a-splashin',
       'Cross the ford o' Kabul river in the dark.

25 Kabul town was ours to take –
    Blow the bugle, draw the sword –
I'd ha' left it for 'is sake –
    'Im that left me by the ford.
       Ford, ford, ford o' Kabul river,
30   Ford o' Kabul river in the dark!
       It's none so bloomin' dry there; ain't you never
          comin' nigh there,
       'Cross the ford o' Kabul river in the dark?

Kabul town'll go to hell –
    Blow the bugle, draw the sword –
35 'Fore I see him 'live an' well –
    'Im the best beside the ford.
       Ford, ford, ford o' Kabul river,
        Ford o' Kabul river in the dark!
       Gawd 'elp 'em if they blunder, for their boots'll pull
          'em under,
40   By the ford o' Kabul river in the dark.

Turn your 'orse from Kabul town –
    Blow the bugle, draw the sword –
'Im an' 'arf my troop is down,
    Down an' drownded by the ford.
      Ford, ford, ford o' Kabul river,
        Ford o' Kabul river in the dark!
      There's the river low an' fallin', but it ain't no use a-
        callin'
        'Cross the ford o' Kabul river in the dark!

45

The English Flag

'Above the portico a flag-staff, bearing the Union Jack, remained
fluttering in the flames for some time, but ultimately when it fell
the crowds rent the air with shouts, and seemed to see significance
in the incident.'

Daily Papers

Winds of the World, give answer! They are whimpering to
    and fro –
And what should they know of England who only England
    know? –
The poor little street-bred people that vapour and fume
    and brag,
They are lifting their heads in the stillness to yelp at the
    English Flag!

Must we borrow a clout from the Boer – to plaster anew
    with dirt?
An Irish liar's bandage, or an English coward's shirt?
We may not speak of England; her Flag's to sell or share.
What is the Flag of England? Winds of the World, declare!

The North Wind blew: – 'From Bergen my steel-shod van-
    guards go;
I chase your lazy whalers home from the Disko floe.

5

10

By the great North Lights above me I work the will of
      God,
And the liner splits on the ice-field or the Dogger fills with
      cod.

I barred my gates with iron, I shuttered my doors with
      flame,
Because to force my ramparts your nutshell navies came.
15   I took the sun from their presence, I cut them down with
      my blast,
And they died, but the Flag of England blew free ere the
      spirit passed.

The lean white bear hath seen it in the long, long Arctic
      nights,
The musk-ox knows the standard that flouts the Northern
      Lights:
What is the Flag of England? Ye have but my bergs to
      dare,
20   Ye have but my drifts to conquer. Go forth, for it is there!'

The South Wind sighed: – 'From the Virgins my mid-sea
      course was ta' en
Over a thousand islands lost in an idle main,
Where the sea-egg flames on the coral and the long-backed
      breakers croon
Their endless ocean legends to the lazy, locked lagoon.

25   Strayed amid lonely islets, mazed amid outer keys,
I waked the palms to laughter – I tossed the scud in the
      breeze.
Never was isle so little, never was sea so lone,
But over the scud and the palm-trees an English flag was
      flown.

I have wrenched it free from the halliards to hang for a
      wisp on the Horn;
30   I have chased it north to the Lizard – ribboned and rolled
      and torn;

I have spread its fold o'er the dying, adrift in a hopeless
        sea;
I have hurled it swift on the slaver, and seen the slave set
        free.

My basking sunfish know it, and wheeling albatross,
Where the lone wave fills with fire beneath the Southern
        Cross.
35   What is the Flag of England? Ye have but my reefs to
        dare,
Ye have but my seas to furrow. Go forth, for it is there!'

The East Wind roared: – 'From the Kuriles, the Bitter
        Seas, I come,
And me men call the Home-Wind, for I bring the English
        home.
Look – look well to your shipping! By the breath of my
        mad typhoon
40   I swept your close-packed Praya and beached your best at
        Kowloon!

The reeling junks behind me and the racing seas before,
I raped your richest roadstead – I plundered Singapore!
I set my hand on the Hugli; as a hooded snake she rose;
And I flung your stoutest steamers to roost with the startled
        crows.

45   Never the lotos closes, never the wild-fowl wake,
But a soul goes out on the East Wind that died for
        England's sake –
Man or woman or suckling, mother or bride or maid –
Because on the bones of the English the English Flag is
        stayed.

The desert-dust hath dimmed it, the flying wild-ass knows,
50   The scared white leopard winds it across the taintless
        snows.
What is the Flag of England? Ye have but my sun to dare,
Ye have but my sands to travel. Go forth, for it is there!'

The West Wind called: 'In squadrons the thoughtless
           galleons fly
That bear the wheat and cattle lest street-bred people die.
55   They make my might their porter, they make my house
           their path,
Till I loose my neck from their rudder and whelm them all
           in my wrath.

I draw the gliding fog-bank as a snake is drawn from the
           hole.
They bellow one to the other, the frighted ship-bells toll;
For day is a drifting terror till I raise the shroud with my
           breath,
60   And they see strange bows above them and the two go
           locked to death.

But whether in calm or wrack-wreath, whether by dark or
           day,
I heave them whole to the conger or rip their plates away,
First of the scattered legions, under a shrieking sky,
Dipping between the rollers, the English Flag goes by.

65   The dead dumb fog hath wrapped it – the frozen dews
           have kissed –
The naked stars have seen it, a fellow-star in the mist.
What is the Flag of England? Ye have but my breath to
           dare,
Ye have but my waves to conquer. Go forth, for it is
           there!'

'The beasts are very wise'

The beasts are very wise,
Their mouths are clean of lies,
They talk one to the other,
Bullock to bullock's brother,

5   Resting after their labours,
     Each in stall with his neighbours.
     But man with goad and whip
     Breaks up their fellowship,
     Shouts in their silky ears,
10   Filling their souls with fears.
     When he has ploughed the land,
     He says: 'They understand.'
     But the beasts in stall together,
     Freed from the yoke and tether,
15   Say as the torn flanks smoke:
     'Nay, 'twas the whip that spoke.'

Cells

I've a head like a concertina: I've a tongue like a button-
                              stick,
I've a mouth like an old potato, and I'm more than a little
                              sick,
But I've had my fun o' the Corp'ral's Guard: I've made
                              the cinders fly,
And I'm here in the Clink for a thundering drink and
                              blacking the Corporal's eye.

5   With a second-hand overcoat under my head,
               And a beautiful view of the yard,
           Oh, it's pack-drill for me and a fortnight's C.B.
               For 'drunk and resisting the Guard!'
               Mad drunk and resisting the Guard –
10   'Strewth, but I socked it them hard!
           So it's pack-drill for me and a fortnight's C.B.
               For 'drunk and resisting the Guard.'

I started o' canteen porter, I finished o' canteen beer,
But a dose o' gin that a mate slipped in, it was that that
                              brought me here.

15 'Twas that and an extry double Guard that rubbed my
                    nose in the dirt –
    But I fell away with the Corp'ral's stock and the best of the
                    Corp'ral's shirt.

    I left my cap in a public-house, my boots in the public road,
    And Lord knows where – and I don't care – my belt and
                    my tunic goed.
    They'll stop my pay, they'll cut away the stripes I used to
                    wear,
20 But I left my mark on the Corp'ral's face, and I think he'll
                    keep it there!

    My wife she cries on the barrack-gate, my kid in the
                    barrack-yard.
    It ain't that I mind the Ord'ly Room – it's *that* that cuts so
                    hard.
    I'll take my oath before them both that I will sure abstain,
    But as soon as I'm in with a mate and gin, I know I'll do it
                    again!

25   With a second-hand overcoat under my head,
              And a beautiful view of the yard,
          Yes, it's pack-drill for me and a fortnight's C.B.
              For 'drunk and resisting the Guard!'
              Mad drunk and resisting the Guard –
30   'Strewth, but I socked it them hard!
          So it's pack-drill for me and a fortnight's C.B.
              For 'drunk and resisting the Guard.'

The Widow's Party

    'Where have you been this while away,
          Johnnie, Johnnie?'
    Out with the rest on a picnic lay.
          Johnnie, my Johnnie, aha!
5   They called us out of the barrack-yard
    To Gawd knows where from Gosport Hard,

And you can't refuse when you get the card,
    And the Widow gives the party.
      (*Bugle*: Ta-rara-ra-ra-rara!)

10 'What did you get to eat and drink,
      Johnnie, Johnnie?'
Standing water as thick as ink,
      Johnnie, my Johnnie, aha!
 A bit o' beef that were three year stored,
15 A bit o' mutton as tough as a board,
And a fowl we killed with a Sergeant's sword,
    When the Widow give the party.

'What did you do for knives and forks,
      Johnnie, Johnnie?'
20 We carries 'em with us wherever we walks,
      Johnnie, my Johnnie, aha!
And some was sliced and some was halved,
And some was crimped and some was carved,
And some was gutted and some was starved,
25   When the Widow give the party.

'What ha' you done with half your mess,
      Johnnie, Johnnie?'
They couldn't do more and they wouldn't do less,
      Johnnie, my Johnnie, aha!
30 They ate their whack and they drank their fill,
And I think the rations has made them ill,
For half my comp'ny's lying still
    Where the Widow give the party.

'How did you get away-away,
35   Johnnie, Johnnie?'
On the broad o' my back at the end o' the day,
      Johnnie, my Johnnie, aha!
I comed away like a bleedin' toff,
For I got four niggers to carry me off,
40 As I lay in the bight of a canvas trough,
    When the Widow give the party.

'What was the end of all the show,
    Johnnie, Johnnie?'
Ask my Colonel, for I don't know,
45   Johnnie, my Johnnie, aha!
We broke a King and we built a road –
A court-house stands where the Reg'ment goed.
And the river's clean where the raw blood flowed
    When the Widow give the party.
50   (*Bugle*: Ta-rara-ra-ra-rara!)

The Exiles' Line

Now the New Year reviving old desires,
The restless soul to open sea aspires,
    Where the Blue Peter flickers from the fore,
And the grimed stoker feeds the engine-fires.

5   Coupons, alas, depart with all their rows,
And last year's sea-met loves where Grindlay knows;
    But still the wild wind wakes off Gardafui,
And hearts turn eastward with the P. & O.'s.

Twelve knots an hour, be they more or less –
10 Oh, slothful mother of much idleness,
    Whom neither rivals spur nor contracts speed!
Nay, bear us gently! Wherefore need we press?

The Tragedy of all our East is laid
On those white decks beneath the awning shade –
15   Birth, absence, longing, laughter, love and tears,
And death unmaking ere the land is made.

And midnight madnesses of souls distraught
Whom the cool seas call through the open port,
    So that the table lacks one place next morn,
20 And for one forenoon men forgo their sport.

The shadow of the rigging to and fro
Sways, shifts, and flickers on the spar-deck's snow,
   And like a giant trampling in his chains,
The screw-blades gasp and thunder deep below;

25 And, leagued to watch one flying-fish's wings,
Heaven stoops to sea, and sea to Heaven clings;
   While, bent upon the ending of his toil,
The hot sun strides, regarding not these things:

For the same wave that meets our stem in spray
30 Bore Smith of Asia eastward yesterday,
   And Delhi Jones and Brown of Midnapore
To-morrow follow on the self-same way.

Linked in the chain of Empire, one by one,
Flushed with long leave, or tanned with many a sun,
35   The Exiles' Line brings out the exiles' line,
And ships them homeward when their work is done.

Yea, heedless of the shuttle through the loom,
The flying keels fulfil the web of doom.
   Sorrow or shouting – what is that to them?
40 Make out the cheque that pays for cabin-room!

And howso many score of times ye flit
With wife and babe and caravan of kit,
   Not all thy travels past shall lower one fare,
Not all thy tears abate one pound of it.

45 And howso high thine earth-born dignity,
Honour and state, go sink it in the sea,
   Till that great One upon the quarter-deck,
Brow-bound with gold, shall give thee leave to be.

Indeed, indeed from that same Line we swear
50 Off for all time, and mean it when we swear;
   And then, and then we meet the Quartered Flag,
And, surely for the last time, pay the fare.

And Green of Kensington, estrayed to view
In three short months the world he never knew,
55   Stares with blind eyes upon the Quartered Flag
And sees no more than yellow, red and blue.

But we, the gipsies of the East, but we –
Waifs of the land and wastrels of the sea –
    Come nearer home beneath the Quartered Flag
60   Than ever home shall come to such as we.

The camp is struck, the bungalow decays,
Dead friends and houses desert mark our ways,
    Till sickness send us down to Prince's Dock
To meet the changeless use of many days.

65   Bound in the wheel of Empire, one by one,
The chain-gangs of the East from sire to son,
    The Exiles' Line takes out the exiles' line
And ships them homeward when their work is done.

How runs the old indictment? 'Dear and slow,'
70   So much and twice so much. We gird, but go.
    For all the soul of our sad East is there,
Beneath the house-flag of the P. & O.!

When Earth's Last Picture is Painted

When Earth's last picture is painted and the tubes are
            twisted and dried,
When the oldest colours have faded, and the youngest
            critic has died,
We shall rest, and, faith, we shall need it – lie down for an
            aeon or two,
Till the Master of All Good Workmen shall put us to work
            anew.

5 And those that were good shall be happy: they shall sit in a
    golden chair;
 They shall splash at a ten-league canvas with brushes of
    comets' hair;
 They shall find real saints to draw from – Magdalene,
    Peter, and Paul;
 They shall work for an age at a sitting and never be tired at
    all!

 And only The Master shall praise us, and only The Master
    shall blame;
10 And no one shall work for money, and no one shall work
    for fame,
 But each for the joy of working, and each, in his separate
    star,
 Shall draw the Thing as he sees It for the God of Things
    as They are!

In the Neolithic Age

In the Neolithic Age savage warfare did I wage
 For food and fame and woolly horses' pelt.
I was singer to my clan in that dim, red Dawn of Man,
 And I sang of all we fought and feared and felt.

5 Yea, I sang as now I sing, when the Prehistoric spring
  Made the piled Biscayan ice-pack split and shove;
 And the troll and gnome and dwerg, and the Gods of Cliff
   and Berg
  Were about me and beneath me and above.

 But a rival of Solutré, told the tribe my style was *outré* –
10 'Neath a tomahawk, of diorite, he fell.
 And I left my views on Art, barbed and tanged, below the
   heart
  Of a mammothistic etcher at Grenelle.

Then I stripped them, scalp from skull, and my hunting-
        dogs fed full,
    And their teeth I threaded neatly on a thong;
15 And I wiped my mouth and said, 'It is well that they are
        dead,
    For I know my work is right and theirs was wrong.'

But my Totem saw the shame; from his ridgepole-shrine
        he came,
    And he told me in a vision of the night: –
'There are nine-and-sixty ways of constructing tribal lays,
20   And every single one of them is right!'

                .   .   .   .   .

Then the silence closed upon me till They put new clothing
        on me
    Of whiter, weaker flesh and bone more frail;
And I stepped beneath Time's finger, once again a tribal
        singer,
    And a minor poet certified by Traill!

25 Still they skirmish to and fro, men my messmates on the
        snow,
    When we headed off the aurochs turn for turn;
When the rich Allobrogenses never kept amanuenses,
    And our only plots were piled in lakes at Berne.

Still a cultured Christian age sees us scuffle, squeak, and
        rage,
30   Still we pinch and slap and jabber, scratch and dirk;
Still we let our business slide – as we dropped the half-
        dressed hide –
    To show a fellow-savage how to work.

Still the world is wondrous large, – seven seas from marge
        to marge –
    And it holds a vast of various kinds of man;
35 And the wildest dreams of Kew are the facts of
        Khatmandhu,
    And the crimes of Clapham chaste in Martaban.

Here's my wisdom for your use, as I learned it when the
moose
And the reindeer roamed where Paris roars to-night:–
'*There are nine-and-sixty ways of constructing tribal lays,*
40   *And-every-single-one-of-them-is-right!*'

The Last Chantey

'And there was no more sea.'

Revelation 21:1

Thus said the Lord in the Vault above the Cherubim,
    Calling to the Angels and the Souls in their degree:
        'Lo! Earth has passed away
        On the smoke of Judgement Day.
5   That Our word may be established shall We gather up
        the Sea?'

Loud sang the souls of the jolly, jolly Mariners:
    'Plague upon the hurricane that made us furl and flee!
        But the war is done between us,
        In the deep the Lord hath seen us –
10   Our bones we'll leave the barracout', and God may sink
        the Sea!'

Then said the soul of Judas that betrayèd Him:
    'Lord, hast Thou forgotten Thy covenant with me?
        How once a year I go
        To cool me on the floe?
15   And Ye take my day of mercy if Ye take away the Sea!'

Then said the soul of the Angel of the Off-shore Wind:
    (He that bits the thunder when the bull-mouthed
        breakers flee):
        'I have watch and ward to keep
        O'er Thy wonders on the deep,
20   And Ye take mine honour from me if Ye take away the Sea!'

Loud sang the souls of the jolly, jolly Mariners:
   'Nay, but we were angry, and a hasty folk are we.
     If we worked the ship together
     Till she foundered in foul weather,
25   Are we babes that we should clamour for a vengeance
       on the Sea?'

Then said the souls of the Slaves that men threw
       overboard:
   'Kennelled in the picaroon a weary band were we;
     But Thy arm was strong to save,
     And it touched us on the wave,
30   And we drowsed the long tides idle till Thy Trumpets
      tore the Sea.'

Then cried the soul of the stout Apostle Paul to God:
   'Once we frapped a ship, and she laboured woundily.
     There were fourteen score of these,
     And they blessed Thee on their knees,
35   When they learned Thy Grace and Glory under Malta
      by the Sea!'

Loud sang the souls of the jolly, jolly Mariners,
   Plucking at their harps, and they plucked unhandily:
     'Our thumbs are rough and tarred,
     And the tune is something hard –
40   May we lift a Deepsea Chantey such as seamen use at
      sea?'

Then said the souls of the Gentlemen-Adventurers –
   Fettered wrist to bar all for red iniquity:
     'Ho, we revel in our chains
     O'er the sorrow that was Spain's!
45   Heave or sink it, leave or drink it, we were masters of
      the Sea!'

Up spake the soul of a grey Gothavn 'speckshioner –
   (He that led the flenching in the fleets of fair Dundee):

'Oh, the ice-blink white and near,
And the bowhead breaching clear!
50   Will Ye whelm them all for wantonness that wallow in
the Sea?'

Loud sang the souls of the jolly, jolly Mariners,
Crying: 'Under Heaven, here is neither lead nor lee!
Must we sing for evermore
On the windless, glassy floor?
55   Take back your golden fiddles and we'll beat to open
sea!'

Then stooped the Lord, and He called the good Sea up to
Him,
And 'stablishèd its borders unto all eternity,
That such as have no pleasure
For to praise the Lord by measure,
60   They may enter into galleons and serve Him on the Sea.

Sun, wind, and cloud shall fail not from the face of it,
Stinging, ringing spindrift, nor the fulmar flying free;
And the ships shall go abroad
To the Glory of the Lord
65   *Who heard the silly sailor-folk and gave them back their*
Sea!

'For to Admire'

The Injian ocean sets an' smiles
So sof', so bright, so bloomin' blue;
There aren't a wave for miles an' miles
Excep' the jiggle from the screw.
5   The ship is swep', the day is done,
The bugle's gone for smoke and play;
An' black ag'in the settin' sun
The Lascar sings, '*Hum deckty hai!*'

For to admire an' for to see,
10   *For to be'old this world so wide –*
It never done no good to me,
      But I can't drop it if I tried!

I see the sergeants pitchin' quoits,
      I 'ear the women laugh an' talk,
15 I spy upon the quarter-deck
      The orficers an' lydies walk.
I thinks about the things that was,
      An' leans an' looks acrost the sea,
Till, spite of all the crowded ship,
20   There's no one lef' alive but me.

The things that was which I 'ave seen,
      In barrick, camp, an' action too,
I tells them over by myself,
      An' sometimes wonders if they're true;
25 For they was odd – most awful odd –
      But all the same, now they are o'er,
There must be 'eaps o' plenty such,
      An' if I wait I'll see some more.

Oh, I 'ave come upon the books,
30   An' frequent broke a barrick-rule,
An' stood beside an' watched myself
      Be'avin' like a bloomin' fool.
I paid my price for findin' out,
      Nor never grutched the price I paid,
35 But sat in Clink without my boots,
      Admirin' 'ow the world was made.

Be'old a cloud upon the beam,
      An' 'umped above the sea appears
Old Aden, like a barrick-stove
40   That no one's lit for years an' years.
I passed by that when I began,
      An' I go 'ome the road I came,
A time-expired soldier-man
      With six years' service to 'is name.

45   My girl she said, 'Oh, stay with me!'
          My mother 'eld me to 'er breast.
      They've never written none, an' so
          They must 'ave gone with all the rest –
      With all the rest which I 'ave seen
50   An' found an' known an' met along.
      I cannot say the things I feel,
          And so I sing my evenin' song:

      For to admire an' for to see,
          For to be' old this world so wide –
55   *It never done no good to me,*
          But I can't drop it if I tried!

The Law of the Jungle

Now this is the Law of the Jungle – as old and as true as the
          sky;
And the Wolf that shall keep it may prosper, but the Wolf
          that shall break it must die.

As the creeper that girdles the tree-trunk the Law runneth
          forward and back –
For the strength of the Pack is the Wolf, and the strength of
          the Wolf is the Pack.

5   Wash daily from nose-tip to tail-tip; drink deeply, but
              never too deep;
      And remember the night is for hunting, and forget not the
              day is for sleep.

      The Jackal may follow the Tiger, but, Cub, when thy
              whiskers are grown,
      Remember the Wolf is a hunter – go forth and get food of
              thine own.

Keep peace with the Lords of the Jungle – the Tiger, the
        Panther, the Bear;
10   And trouble not Hathi the Silent, and mock not the Boar
        in his lair.

When Pack meets with Pack in the Jungle, and neither will
        go from the trail,
Lie down till the leaders have spoken – it may be fair
        words shall prevail.

When ye fight with a Wolf of the Pack, ye must fight him
        alone and afar,
Lest others take part in the quarrel, and the Pack be
        diminished by war.

15   The Lair of the Wolf is his refuge, and where he has made
        him his home,
Not even the Head Wolf may enter, not even the Council
        may come.

The Lair of the Wolf is his refuge, but where he has
        digged it too plain,
The Council shall send him a message, and so he shall
        change it again.

If ye kill before midnight, be silent, and wake not the
        woods with your bay,
20   Lest ye frighten the deer from the crops, and the brothers
        go empty away.

Ye may kill for yourselves, and your mates, and your cubs
        as they need, and ye can;
But kill not for pleasure of killing, and *seven times never kill
        Man!*

If ye plunder his Kill from a weaker, devour not all in thy
        pride;
Pack-Right is the right of the meanest; so leave him the
        head and the hide.

25 The Kill of the Pack is the meat of the Pack. Ye must eat
        where it lies;
    And no one may carry away of that meat to his lair, or he dies.

    The Kill of the Wolf is the meat of the Wolf. He may do
        what he will,
    But, till he has given permission, the Pack may not eat of
        that Kill.

    Cub-Right is the right of the Yearling. From all of his Pack
        he may claim
30 Full-gorge when the killer has eaten; and none may refuse
        him the same.

    Lair-Right is the right of the Mother. From all of her year
        she may claim
    One haunch of each kill for her litter; and none may deny
        her the same.

    Cave-Right is the right of the Father – to hunt by himself
        for his own:
    He is freed of all calls to the Pack; he is judged by the
        Council alone.

35 Because of his age and his cunning, because of his gripe
        and his paw,
    In all that the Law leaveth open, the word of the Head
        Wolf is Law.

    *Now these are the Laws of the Jungle, and many and mighty
        are they;*
    *But the head and the hoof of the Law and the haunch and the
        hump is – Obey!*

The Three-Decker

1894

'The three-volume novel is extinct.'

Full thirty foot she towered from waterline to rail.
It took a watch to steer her, and a week to shorten sail;
But, 'spite all modern notions, I've found her first and
    best –
The only certain packet for the Islands of the Blest.

5   Fair held the breeze behind us – 'twas warm with lovers'
    prayers.
We'd stolen wills for ballast and a crew of missing heirs.
They shipped as Able Bastards till the Wicked Nurse
    confessed,
And they worked the old three-decker to the Islands of the
    Blest.

By ways no gaze could follow, a course unspoiled of Cook,
10   Per Fancy, fleetest in man, our titled berths we took,
With maids of matchless beauty and parentage unguessed,
And a Church of England parson for the Islands of the
    Blest.

We asked no social questions – we pumped no hidden
    shame –
We never talked obstetrics when the Little Stranger
    came:
15   We left the Lord in Heaven, we left the fiends in Hell.
We weren't exactly Yussufs, but – Zuleika didn't tell.

No moral doubt assailed us, so when the port we neared,
The villain had his flogging at the gangway, and we
    cheered.
'Twas fiddle in the foc'sle – 'twas garlands on the mast,
20   For every one got married, and I went ashore at last.

I left 'em all in couples a-kissing on the decks.
I left the lovers loving and the parents signing cheques.
In endless English comfort, by county-folk caressed,
I left the old three-decker at the Islands of the Blest! . . .

25 That route is barred to steamers: you'll never lift again
    Our purple-painted headlands or the lordly keeps of
                Spain.
They're just beyond your skyline, however far you cruise
    In a ram-you-damn-you liner with a brace of bucking
                screws.

Swing round your aching searchlight – 'twill show no
                haven's peace.
30 Ay, blow your shrieking sirens at the deaf, grey-bearded
                seas!
Boom out the dripping oil-bags to skin the deep's unrest –
And you aren't one knot the nearer to the Islands of the
                Blest!

But when you're threshing, crippled, with broken bridge
                and rail,
At a drogue of dead convictions to hold you head to gale,
35 Calm as the Flying Dutchman, from truck to taffrail
                dressed,
You'll see the old three-decker for the Islands of the Blest.

You'll see her tiering canvas in sheeted silver spread;
You'll hear the long-drawn thunder 'neath her leaping
                figurehead;
While far, so far above you, her tall poop-lanterns shine
40 Unvexed by wind or weather like the candles round a
                shrine.

Hull down – hull down and under – she dwindles to a
                speck,
With noise of pleasant music and dancing on her deck.
All's well – all's well aboard her – she's left you far behind,
With a scent of old-world roses through the fog that ties
                you blind.

45   Her crew are babes or madmen? Her port is all to make?
      You're manned by Truth and Science, and you steam for
                steaming's sake?
      Well, tinker up your engines – you know your business
                best –
      She's taking tired people to the Islands of the Blest!

'Back to the Army Again'

I'm 'ere in a ticky ulster an' a broken billycock 'at,
A-laying on to the Sergeant I don't know a gun from a bat;
My shirt's doin' duty for jacket, my sock's stickin' out o'
                my boots,
An' I'm learnin' the damned old goose-step along o' the
                new recruits!

5   Back to the Army again, Sergeant,
                Back to the Army again.
              Don't look so 'ard, for I 'aven't no card,
                I'm back to the Army again!

      I done my six years' service. 'Er Majesty sez: 'Good day –
10   You'll please to come when you're rung for, an' 'ere's your
                ole back-pay;
      An' fourpence a day for baccy – an' bloomin' gen'rous, too;
      An' now you can make your fortune – the same as your
                orf'cers do.'

              Back to the Army again, Sergeant,
                Back to the Army again.
15   'Ow did I learn to do right-about-turn?
                I'm back to the Army again!

      A man o' four-an'-twenty that 'asn't learned of a trade –
      Beside 'Reserve' agin' him – 'e'd better be never made.
      I tried my luck for a quarter, an' that was enough for me,
20   An' I thought of 'Er Majesty's barricks, an' I thought I'd
                go an' see.

> Back to the Army again, Sergeant,
> Back to the Army again.
> 'Tisn't my fault if I dress when I 'alt –
> I'm back to the Army again!

25 The Sergeant arst no questions, but 'e winked the other
            eye,
    'E sez to me, "'Shun!" an' I shunted, the same as in days
            gone by;
    For 'e saw the set o' my shoulders, an' I couldn't 'elp
            'oldin' straight
    When me an' the other rookies come under the barrick-
            gate.

> Back to the Army again, Sergeant,
30 > Back to the Army again.
> 'Oo would ha' thought I could carry an' port?
> I'm back to the Army again!

    I took my bath, an' I wallered – for, Gawd, I needed it so!
    I smelt the smell o' the barricks, I 'eard the bugles go.
35 I 'eard the feet on the gravel – the feet o' the men what
            drill –
    An' I sez to my flutterin' 'eart-strings, I sez to 'em, 'Peace,
            be still!'

> Back to the Army again, Sergeant,
> Back to the Army again.
> 'Oo said I knew when the troopship was due?
40 > I'm back to the Army again!

    I carried my slops to the tailor; I sez to 'im, 'None o' your
            lip!
    You tight 'em over the shoulders, an' loose 'em over the
            'ip,
    For the set o' the tunic's 'orrid.' An' 'e sez to me, 'Strike
            me dead,
    But I thought you was used to the business!' an' so 'e done
            what I said.

45   Back to the Army again, Sergeant,
            Back to the Army again.
        Rather too free with my fancies? Wot – me?
            I'm back to the Army again!

        Next week I'll 'ave 'em fitted; I'll buy me a swagger-cane;
50   They'll let me free o' the barricks to walk on the Hoe
                again,
        In the name o' William Parsons, that used to be Edward
                Clay,
        An' – any pore beggar that wants it can draw my fourpence
                a day!

        Back to the Army again, Sergeant,
            Back to the Army again.
55   Out o' the cold an' the rain, Sergeant,
            Out o' the cold an' the rain.
                        'Oo's there?

        A man that's too good to be lost you,
            A man that is 'andled an' made –
60   A man that will pay what 'e cost you
            In learnin' the others their trade – parade!
        You're droppin' the pick o' the Army
            Because you don't 'elp 'em remain,
        But drives 'em to cheat to get out o' the street
65   An' back to the Army again!

Road-Song of the Bandar-Log

        Here we go in a flung festoon,
        Half-way up to the jealous moon!
        Don't you envy our pranceful bands?
        Don't you wish you had extra hands?
5   Wouldn't you like if your tails were – *so* –
        Curved in the shape of a Cupid's bow?
            Now you're angry, but – never mind,
            Brother, thy tail hangs down behind!

Here we sit in a branchy row,
10   Thinking of beautiful things we know;
Dreaming of deeds that we mean to do,
All complete, in a minute or two –
Something noble and grand and good,
Won by merely wishing we could.
15   Now we're going to – never mind,
          Brother, thy tail hangs down behind!

All the talk we ever have heard
Uttered by bat or beast or bird –
Hide or fin or scale or feather –
20   Jabber it quickly and all together!
Excellent! Wonderful! Once again!
Now we are talking just like men.
          Let's pretend we are . . . Never mind!
          Brother, thy tail hangs down behind!
25   This is the way of the Monkey-kind!

Then join our leaping lines that scumfish through the pines,
That rocket by where, light and high, the wild-grape swings.
By the rubbish in our wake, and the noble noise we make,
Be sure – be sure, we're going to do some splendid things!

McAndrew's Hymn

Lord, Thou hast made this world below the shadow of a
          dream,
An', taught by time, I tak' it so – exceptin' always Steam.
From coupler-flange to spindle-guide I see Thy Hand, O
          God –
Predestination in the stride o' yon connectin'-rod.
5   John Calvin might ha' forged the same – enormous, certain,
          slow –
Ay, wrought it in the furnace-flame – *my* 'Institutio.'
I cannot get my sleep to-night; old bones are hard to
          please;

I'll stand the middle watch up here – alone wi' God an'
    these
My engines, after ninety days o' race an' rack an' strain
10 Through all the seas of all Thy world, slam-bangin' home
    again.
Slam-bang too much – they knock a wee – the crosshead-
    gibs are loose,
But thirty thousand mile o' sea has gied them fair
    excuse . . .
Fine, clear an' dark – a full-draught breeze, wi' Ushant out
    o' sight,
An' Ferguson relievin' Hay. Old girl, ye'll walk to-night!
15 His wife's at Plymouth . . . Seventy – One – Two – Three
    since he began –
Three turns for Mistress Ferguson . . . and who's to blame
    the man?
There's none at any port for me, by drivin' fast or slow,
Since Elsie Campbell went to Thee, Lord, thirty years ago.
(The year the *Sarah Sands* was burned. Oh, roads we used
    to tread,
20 Fra' Maryhill to Pollokshaws – fra' Govan to Parkhead!)
Not but they're ceevil on the Board. Ye'll hear Sir Kenneth
    say:
'Good morrn, McAndrew! Back again? An' how's your
    bilge to-day?'
Miscallin' technicalities but handin' me my chair
To drink Madeira wi' three Earls – the auld Fleet Engineer
25 That started as a boiler-whelp – when steam and he were
    low.
I mind the time we used to serve a broken pipe wi' tow!
Ten pound was all the pressure then – Eh! Eh! – a man
    wad drive;
An' here, our workin' gauges give one hunder sixty-five!
We're creepin' on wi' each new rig – less weight an' larger
    power;
30 There'll be the loco-boiler next an' thirty mile an' hour!
Thirty an' more. What I ha' seen since ocean-steam began
Leaves me na doot for the machine: but what about the
    man?

The man that counts, wi' all his runs, one million mile
        o'sea:
Four time the span from earth to moon . . . How far, O
        Lord, from Thee
35   That wast beside him night an' day? Ye mind my first
        typhoon?
It scoughed the skipper on his way to jock wi' the saloon.
Three feet were on the stokehold-floor – just slappin' to
        an' fro –
An' cast me on a furnace-door. I have the marks to show.
Marks! I ha' marks o' more than burns – deep in my soul
        an' black,
40   An' times like this, when things go smooth, my wickudness
        comes back.
The sins o' four an' forty years, all up an' down the seas,
Clack an' repeat like valves half-fed . . . Forgie's our
        trespasses!
Nights when I'd come on deck to mark, wi' envy in my
        gaze,
The couples kittlin' in the dark between the funnel-stays;
45   Years when I raked the Ports wi' pride to fill my cup o'
        wrong –
Judge not, O Lord, my steps aside at Gay Street in Hong-
        Kong!
Blot out the wastrel hours of mine in sin, when I abode –
Jane Harrigan's an' Number Nine, The Reddick an' Grant
        Road!
An' waur than all – my crownin' sin – rank blasphemy an' wild.
50   I wasna four and twenty then – Ye wadna judge a child?
I'd seen the Tropics first that run – new fruit, new smells,
        new air –
How could I tell – blind-fou wi' sun – the Deil was lurkin'
        there?
By day like playhouse-scenes the shore slid past our sleepy
        eyes;
By night those soft, lasceevious stars leered from those
        velvet skies,
55   In port (we used no cargo-steam) I'd daunder down the
        streets –

An ijjit grinnin' in a dream – for shells an' parrakeets,
An' walkin'-sticks o' carved bamboo an' blowfish stuffed
    an' dried –
Fillin' my bunk wi' rubbishry the Chief put overside,
Till, off Sambawa Head, Ye mind, I heard a land-breeze
    ca',
60 Milk-warm wi' breath o' spice an' bloom: 'McAndrew,
    come awa'!'
Firm, clear an' low – no haste, no hate – the ghostly
    whisper went,
Just statin' eevidential facts beyon' all argument:
'Your mither's God's a graspin' deil, the shadow o'
    yoursel',
Got out o' books by meenisters clean daft on Heaven an'
    Hell.
65 They mak' him in the Broomielaw, o' Glasgie cold an' dirt,
A jealous, pridefu' fetish, lad, that's only strong to hurt.
Ye'll not go back to Him again an' kiss His red-hot rod,
But come wi' Us' (Now, who were *They*?) 'an' know the
    Leevin' God,
That does not kipper souls for sport or break a life in jest,
70 But swells the ripenin' cocoanuts an' ripes the woman's
    breast.'
An' there it stopped – cut off – no more – that quiet,
    certain voice –
For me, six months o' twenty-four, to leave or take at
    choice.
'Twas on me like a thunderclap – it racked me through an'
    through –
Temptation past the show o' speech, unnameable an' new –
75 The Sin against the Holy Ghost? . . . An' under all, our
    screw.

That storm blew by but left behind her anchor-shiftin'
    swell.
Thou knowest all my heart an' mind, Thou knowest, Lord,
    I fell –
Third on the *Mary Gloster* then, and first that night in
    Hell!

Yet was Thy Hand beneath my head, about my feet Thy
    Care –
80 Fra' Deli clear to Torres Strait, the trial o' despair,
But when we touched the Barrier Reef Thy answer to my
    prayer! . . .
We daredna run that sea by night but lay an' held our fire,
An' I was drowsin' on the hatch – sick – sick wi' doubt an'
    tire:
'Better the sight of eyes that see than wanderin' o' desire!'
85 Ye mind that word? Clear as our gongs – again, an' once
    again,
When rippin' down through coral-trash ran out our
    moorin'-chain:
An', by Thy Grace, I had the Light to see my duty plain.
Light on the engine-room – no more – bright as our
    carbons burn.
I've lost it since a thousand times, but never past return!

    . . . . .

90 Obsairve! Per annum we'll have here two thousand souls
    aboard –
Think not I dare to justify myself before the Lord,
But – average fifteen hunder souls safe-borne fra' port to
    port –
I *am* o' service to my kind. Ye wadna blame the thought?
Maybe they steam from Grace to Wrath – to sin by folly
    led –
95 It isna mine to judge their path – their lives are on my
    head.
Mine at the last – when all is done it all comes back to me,
The fault that leaves six thousand ton a log upon the sea.
We'll tak' one stretch – three weeks an' odd by ony road ye
    steer –
Fra' Cape Town east to Wellington – ye need an engineer.
100 Fail there – ye've time to weld your shaft – ay, eat it, ere
    ye're spoke;
Or make Kerguelen under sail – three jiggers burned wi'
    smoke!
An' home again – the Rio run: it's no child's play to go

Steamin' to bell for fourteen days o' snow an' floe an'
blow.

The bergs like kelpies overside that girn an' turn an' shift

105   Whaur, grindin' like the Mills o' God, goes by the big
South drift.

(Hail, Snow and Ice that praise the Lord. I've met them at
their work,

An' wished we had anither route or they anither kirk.)

Yon's strain, hard strain, o' head an' hand, for though Thy
Power brings

All skill to naught, Ye'll understand a man must think o'
things.

110   Then, at the last, we'll get to port an' hoist their baggage
clear —

The passengers, wi' gloves an' canes — an' this is what I'll
hear:

'Well, thank ye for a pleasant voyage. The tender's comin'
now.'

While I go testin' follower-bolts an' watch the skipper bow.

They've words for every one but me — shake hands wi' half
the crew,

115   Except the dour Scots engineer, the man they never knew.

An' yet I like the wark for all we've dam'-few pickin's
here —

No pension, an' the most we'll earn's four hunder pound a
year.

Better myself abroad? Maybe. *I'd* sooner starve than sail
Wi' such as call a snifter-rod *ross* . . . French for
nightingale.

120   Commeesion on my stores? Some do; but I cannot afford
To lie like stewards wi' patty-pans. I'm older than the
Board.

A bonus on the coal I save? Ou ay, the Scots are close,
But when I grudge the strength Ye gave I'll grudge their
food to *those*.

(There's bricks that I might recommend — an' clink the
fire-bars cruel.

125   No! Welsh — Wangarti at the worst — an' damn all patent
fuel!)

Inventions? Ye must stay in port to mak' a patent pay.

My Deeferential Valve-Gear taught me how that business lay.

I blame no chaps wi' clearer heads for aught they make or sell.

I found that I could not invent an' look to these as well.

130 So, wrestled wi' Apollyon – Nah! – fretted like a bairn –

But burned the workin'-plans last run, wi' all I hoped to earn.

Ye know how hard an Idol dies, an' what that meant to me –

E'en tak' it for a sacrifice acceptable to Thee . . .

Below there! Oiler! What's your wark? Ye find it runnin' hard?

135 *Ye needn't swill the cup wi' oil – this isn't the Cunard!*

Ye thought? Ye are not paid to think. Go, sweat that off again!

Tck! Tck! It's deeficult to sweer nor tak' The Name in vain!

Men, ay, an' women, call me stern. Wi' these to oversee,

Ye'll note I've little time to burn on social repartee.

140 The bairns see what their elders miss; they'll hunt me to an' fro,

Till for the sake of – well, a kiss – I tak' 'em down below.

That minds me of our Viscount loon – Sir Kenneth's kin – the chap

Wi' Russia-leather tennis-shoon an' spar-decked yachtin'-cap.

I showed him round last week, o'er all – an' at the last says he:

145 'Mister McAndrew, don't you think steam spoils romance at sea?'

Damned ijjit! I'd been doon that morn to see what ailed the throws,

Manholin', on my back – the cranks three inches off my nose.

Romance! Those first-class passengers they like it very well,

Printed an' bound in little books; but why don't poets tell?

150 I'm sick of all their quirks an' turns – the loves an' doves
          they dream –
    Lord, send a man like Robbie Burns to sing the Song o'
          Steam!
    To match wi' Scotia's noblest speech yon orchestra sublime
    Whaurto – uplifted like the Just – the tail-rods mark the
          time.
    The crank-throws give the double-bass, the feed-pump
          sobs an' heaves,
155 An' now the main eccentrics start their quarrel on the
          sheaves:
    Her time, her own appointed time, the rocking link-head
          bides,
    Till – hear that note? – the rod's return whings glimmerin'
          through the guides.
    They're all awa'! True beat, full power, the clangin' chorus
          goes
    Clear to the tunnel where they sit, my purrin' dynamoes.
160 Interdependence absolute, foreseen, ordained, decreed,
    To work, Ye'll note, at ony tilt an' every rate o' speed.
    Fra' skylight-lift to furnace-bars, backed, bolted, braced
          an' stayed,
    An' singin' like the Mornin' Stars for joy that they are
          made;
    While, out o' touch o' vanity, the sweatin' thrust-block
          says:
165 'Not unto us the praise, or man – not unto us the praise!'
    Now, a' together, hear them lift their lesson – theirs an'
          mine:
    'Law, Orrder, Duty an' Restraint, Obedience, Discipline!'
    Mill, forge an' try-pit taught them that when roarin' they
          arose,
    An' whiles I wonder if a soul was gied them wi' the blows.
170 Oh for a man to weld it then, in one trip-hammer strain,
    Till even first-class passengers could tell the meanin' plain!
    But no one cares except mysel' that serve an' understand
    My seven thousand horse-power here. Eh, Lord! They're
          grand – they're grand!
    Uplift am I? When first in store the new-made beasties stood,

175   Were Ye cast down that breathed the Word declarin' all
               things good?
    Not so! O' that warld-liftin' joy no after-fall could vex,
    Ye've left a glimmer still to cheer the Man – the
               Arrtifex!
    That holds, in spite o' knock and scale, o' friction, waste
               an' slip,
    An' by that light – now, mark my word – we'll build the
               Perfect Ship.
180   I'll never last to judge her lines or take her curve – not I.
    But I ha' lived an' I ha' worked. Be thanks to Thee, Most
               High!
    An' I ha' done what I ha' done – judge Thou if ill or
               well –
    Always Thy Grace preventin' me . . .
                      Losh! Yon's the 'Stand-by' bell.
185   Pilot so soon? His flare it is. The mornin'-watch is set.
    Well, God be thanked, as I was sayin', I'm no Pelagian
               yet.
    Now I'll tak' on . . .
      'Morrn, Ferguson. Man, have ye ever thought
    What your good leddy costs in coal? . . . I'll burn 'em down to
      port.

'The Men that fought at Minden'

(IN THE LODGE OF INSTRUCTION)

The men that fought at Minden, they was rookies in their
      time –
  So was them that fought at Waterloo!
All the 'ole command, yuss, from Minden to Maiwand,
  They was once dam' sweeps like you!

5   *Then do not be discouraged, 'Eaven is your 'elper,*
    We'll learn you not to forget;
  An' you mustn't swear an' curse, or you'll only catch it worse,
    For we'll make you soldiers yet!

The men that fought at Minden, they 'ad stocks beneath
         their chins,
10   Six inch 'igh an' more;
But fatigue it was their pride, an' they *would* not be denied
    To clean the cook-'ouse floor.

The men that fought at Minden, they had anarchistic
         bombs
    Served to 'em by name of 'and grenades;
15   But they got it in the eye (same as you will by an' by)
    When they clubbed their field-parades.

The men that fought at Minden, they 'ad buttons up an'
         down,
    Two-an'-twenty dozen of 'em told;
But they didn't grouse an' shirk at an hour's extry work,
20   They kept 'em bright as gold.

The men that fought at Minden, they was armed with
         musketoons,
    Also, they was drilled by 'alberdiers.
I don't know what they were, but the sergeants took good
         care
    They washed be'ind their ears.

25   The men that fought at Minden, they 'ad ever cash in 'and
    Which they did not bank nor save,
But spent it gay an' free on their betters – such as me –
    For the good advice I gave.

The men that fought at Minden, they was civil – yuss, they
         was –
30   Never didn't talk o' rights an' wrongs,
But they got it with the toe (same as you will get it – so!) –
    For interrupting songs.

The men that fought at Minden, they was several other
         things
    Which I don't remember clear;

35   But *that's* the reason why, now the six-year men are dry,
    The rooks will stand the beer!

  Then do not be discouraged, 'Eaven is your 'elper,
    We'll learn you not to forget;
  An' you mustn't swear an' curse, or you'll only catch it worse,
40   *An' we'll make you soldiers yet!*

  Soldiers yet, if you've got it in you –
    All for the sake of the Core;
  Soldiers yet, if we 'ave to skin you –
    Run an' get the beer, Johnny Raw – Johnny Raw!
45   *Ho! run an' get the beer, Johnny Raw!*

'The stream is shrunk – the pool is dry'

The stream is shrunk – the pool is dry,
And we be comrades, thou and I;
With fevered jowl and dusty flank
Each jostling each along the bank;
5   And, by one drouthy fear made still,
Forgoing thought of quest or kill.
Now 'neath his dam the fawn may see
The lean Pack-wolf as cowed as he,
And the tall buck, unflinching, note
10 The fangs that tore his father's throat.
The pools are shrunk – the streams are dry,
And we be playmates, thou and I,
Till yonder cloud – Good Hunting! – loose
The rain that breaks our Water Truce.

'The 'Eathen'

The 'eathen in 'is blindness bows down to wood an' stone;
'E don't obey no orders unless they is 'is own;
'E keeps 'is side-arms awful: 'e leaves 'em all about,
An' then comes up the Regiment an' pokes the 'eathen
out.

5   *All along o' dirtiness, all along o' mess,*
       All along o' doin' things rather-more-or-less,
       All along of abby-nay, kul, an' hazar-ho,
       Mind you keep your rifle an' yourself jus' so!

The young recruit is 'aughty – 'e draf's from Gawd knows
where;
10   They bid 'im show 'is stockin's an' lay 'is mattress square;
'E calls it bloomin' nonsense – 'e doesn't know no more –
An' then up comes 'is Company an' kicks 'im round the
floor!

The young recruit is 'ammered – 'e takes it very 'ard;
'E 'angs 'is 'ead an' mutters – 'e sulks about the yard;
15   'E talks o' 'cruel tyrants' which 'e'll swing for by-an'-by,
An' the others 'ears an' mocks 'im, an' the boy goes orf to
cry.

The young recruit is silly – 'e thinks o' suicide.
'E's lost 'is gutter-devil; 'e 'asn't got 'is pride;
But day by day they kicks 'im, which 'elps 'im on a bit,
20   Till 'e finds 'isself one mornin' with a full an' proper
kit.

       Gettin' clear o' dirtiness, gettin' done with mess,
       Gettin' shut o' doin' things rather-more-or-less;
       Not so fond of abby-nay, kul, nor hazar-ho,
       Learns to keep 'is rifle an' 'isself jus' so!

25   The young recruit is 'appy – 'e throws a chest to suit;
You see 'im grow mustaches; you 'ear 'im slap 'is boot.

'E learns to drop the 'bloodies' from every word 'e
        slings,
An' 'e shows an 'ealthy brisket when 'e strips for bars an'
        rings.

The cruel-tyrant-Sergeants they watch 'im 'arf a year;
30   They watch 'im with 'is comrades, they watch 'im with 'is
        beer;
They watch 'im with the women at the Regimental dance,
An' the cruel-tyrant-Sergeants send 'is name along for
        'Lance.'

An' now 'e's 'arf o' nothin', an' all a private yet,
'Is room they up an' rags 'im to see what they will get.
35   They rags 'im low an' cunnin', each dirty trick they can,
But 'e learns to sweat 'is temper an' 'e learns to sweat 'is
        man.

An', last, a Colour-Sergeant, as such to be obeyed,
'E schools 'is men at cricket, 'e tells 'em on parade;
They sees 'im quick an' 'andy, uncommon set an' smart,
40   An' so 'e talks to orficers which 'ave the Core at 'eart.

'E learns to do 'is watchin' without it showin' plain;
'E learns to save a dummy, an' shove 'im straight again;
'E learns to check a ranker that's buyin' leave to shirk;
An 'e learns to make men like 'im so they'll learn to like
        their work.

45   An' when it comes to marchin' he'll see their socks are
        right,
An' when it comes to action 'e shows 'em how to sight.
'E knows their ways of thinkin' and just what's in their
        mind;
'E knows when they are takin' on an' when they've fell
        be'ind.

'E knows each talkin' corp'ral that leads a squad astray;
50   'E feels 'is innards 'eavin', 'is bowels givin' way;

'E sees the blue-white faces all tryin' 'ard to grin,
An ʹe stands anʹ waits anʹ suffers till itʹs time to cap ʹem in.

An' now the hugly bullets come peckin' through the dust,
An' no one wants to face 'em, but every beggar must;
55   So, like a man in irons, which isn't glad to go,
They moves 'em off by companies uncommon stiff an'
            slow.

Of all 'is five years' schoolin' they don't remember much
Excep' the not retreatin', the step an' keepin' touch.
It looks like teachin' wasted when they duck an' spread an'
            'op –
60   But if 'e 'adn't learned 'em they'd be all about the shop!

An' now it's "Oo goes backward?' an' now it's "Oo comes on?'
And now it's 'Get the *doolies*,' an' now the Captain's gone;
An' now it's bloody murder, but all the while they 'ear
'Is voice, the same as barrick-drill, a-shepherdin' the rear.

65   'E's just as sick as they are, 'is 'eart is like to split.
But 'e works 'em, works 'em, works 'em till he feels 'em
            take the bit;
The rest is 'oldin' steady till the watchful bugles play,
An' 'e lifts 'em, lifts 'em, lifts 'em through the charge that
            wins the day!

The 'eathen in 'is blindness bows down to wood an' stone;
70   *'E don't obey no orders unless they is 'is own.*
The 'eathen in 'is blindness must end where 'e began,
But the backbone of the Army is the Non-commissioned
            man!

Keep away from dirtiness – keep away from mess,
Don't get into doin' things rather-more-or-less!
75   *Let's ha' done with* abby-nay, kul, *and* hazar-ho;
Mind you keep your rifle an' yourself jus' so!

The King

'Farewell, Romance!' the Cave-men said;
   'With bone well carved He went away.
Flint arms the ignoble arrowhead,
   And jasper tips the spear to-day.
5 Changed are the Gods of Hunt and Dance,
And He with these. Farewell, Romance!'

'Farewell, Romance!' the Lake-folk sighed;
   'We lift the weight of flatling years;
The caverns of the mountain-side
10   Hold Him who scorns our hutted piers.
Lost hills whereby we dare not dwell,
Guard ye His rest. Romance, Farewell!'

'Farewell, Romance!' the Soldier spoke;
   'By sleight of sword we may not win,
15 But scuffle 'mid uncleanly smoke
     Of arquebus and culverin.
Honour is lost, and none may tell
Who paid good blows. Romance, farewell!'

'Farewell, Romance!' the Traders cried;
20   'Our keels have lain with every sea.
The dull-returning wind and tide
     Heave up the wharf where we would be;
The known and noted breezes swell
Our trudging sails. Romance, farewell!'

25 'Goodbye, Romance!' the Skipper said;
   'He vanished with the coal we burn.
Our dial marks full-steam ahead,
     Our speed is timed to half a turn.
Sure as the ferried barge we ply
30 'Twixt port and port. Romance, good-bye!'

'Romance!' the season-tickets mourn,
    '*He* never ran to catch his train,
But passed with coach and guard and horn –
    And left the agent – Late again!
35   Confound Romance!' . . . And all unseen
Romance brought up the nine-fifteen.

His hand was on the lever laid,
    His oil-can soothed the worrying cranks,
His whistle waked the snowbound grade,
40   His fog-horn cut the reeking Banks;
By dock and deep and mine and mill
The Boy-god reckless laboured still!

Robed, crowned and throned, He wove His spell,
    Where heart-blood beat or hearth-smoke curled,
45 With unconsidered miracle,
    Hedged in a backward-gazing world:
Then taught His chosen bard to say:
'Our King was with us – yesterday!'

The Derelict

'And reports the derelict *Margaret Pollock* still at sea.'
                                        Shipping News

I was the staunchest of our fleet
    Till the sea rose beneath my feet
Unheralded, in hatred past all measure.
    Into his pits he stamped my crew,
5   *Buffeted, blinded, bound and threw,*
Bidding me eyeless wait upon his pleasure.

    Man made me, and my will
    Is to my maker still,
Whom now the currents con, the rollers steer –
10   Lifting forlorn to spy
    Trailed smoke along the sky,
Falling afraid lest any keel come near!

     Wrenched as the lips of thirst,
     Wried, dried, and split and burst,
15 Bone-bleached my decks, wind-scoured to the graining;
     And, jarred at every roll,
     The gear that was my soul
Answers the anguish of my beams' complaining.

     For life that crammed me full,
20   Gangs of the prying gull
That shriek and scrabble on the riven hatches.
     For roar that dumbed the gale,
     My hawse-pipes' guttering wail,
Sobbing my heart out through the uncounted watches.

25   Blind in the hot blue ring
     Through all my points I swing –
Swing and return to shift the sun anew.
     Blind in my well-known sky
     I hear the stars go by,
30 Mocking the prow that cannot hold one true.

     White on my wasted path
     Wave after wave in wrath
Frets 'gainst his fellow, warring where to send me.
     Flung forward, heaved aside,
35   Witless and dazed I bide
The mercy of the comber that shall end me.

     North where the bergs careen,
     The spray of seas unseen
Smokes round my head and freezes in the falling.
40   South where the corals breed,
     The footless, floating weed
Folds me and fouls me, strake on strake upcrawling.

     I that was clean to run
     My race against the sun –
45 Strength on the deep – am bawd to all disaster;

Whipped forth by night to meet
  My sister's careless feet,
And with a kiss betray her to my master.

    Man made me, and my will
50   Is to my maker still –
To him and his, our peoples at their pier:
    Lifting in hope to spy
    Trailed smoke along the sky,
Falling afraid lest any keel come near!

'When 'Omer smote 'is bloomin' lyre'

When 'Omer smote 'is bloomin' lyre,
  'E'd 'eard men sing by land an' sea;
An' what 'e thought 'e might require,
  'E went an' took – the same as me!

5 The market-girls an' fishermen,
    The shepherds an' the sailors, too,
They 'eard old songs turn up again,
    But kep' it quiet -- same as you!

They knew 'e stole; 'e knew they knowed.
10   They didn't tell, nor make a fuss.
But winked at 'Omer down the road,
    An' 'e winked back – the same as us!

The Ladies

I've taken my fun where I've found it;
    I've rogued an' I've ranged in my time;
I've 'ad my pickin' o' sweethearts,
    An' four o' the lot was prime.
5 One was an 'arf-caste widow,

One was a woman at Prome,
One was the wife of a *jemadar-sais*,
    An' one is a girl at 'ome.

Now I aren't no 'and with the ladies,
10   *For, takin' 'em all along,*
You never can say till you've tried 'em,
    An' then you are like to be wrong.
There's times when you'll think that you mightn't,
    There's times when you'll know that you might;
15 *But the things you will learn from the Yellow an' Brown*
    They'll 'elp you a lot with the White!

I was a young un at 'Oogli,
    Shy as a girl to begin;
Aggie de Castrer she made me,
20   An' Aggie was clever as sin;
Older than me, but my first un –
    More like a mother she were –
Showed me the way to promotion an' pay,
    An' I learned about women from 'er!

25 Then I was ordered to Burma,
    Actin' in charge o' Bazar,
An' I got me a tiddy live 'eathen
    Through buyin' supplies off 'er pa.
Funny an' yellow an' faithful –
30   Doll in a teacup she were –
But we lived on the square, like a true-married pair,
    An' I learned about women from 'er!

Then we was shifted to Neemuch
    (Or I might ha' been keepin' 'er now),
35 An' I took with a shiny she-devil,
    The wife of a nigger at Mhow;
Taught me the gipsy-folks' *bolee*;
    Kind o' volcano she were,
For she knifed me one night 'cause I wished she was white,
40   And I learned about women from 'er!

Then I come 'ome in a trooper,
  'Long of a kid o' sixteen –
Girl from a convent at Meerut,
  The straightest I ever 'ave seen.

45 Love at first sight was 'er trouble,
  She didn't know what it were;
An' I wouldn't do such, 'cause I liked 'er too much,
  But – I learned about women from 'er!

I've taken my fun where I've found it,
50 An' now I must pay for my fun,
For the more you 'ave known o' the others
  The less will you settle to one;
An' the end of it's sittin' an' thinkin',
  An' dreamin' Hell-fires to see;
55 So be warned by my lot (which I know you will not),
  An' learn about women from me!

What did the Colonel's Lady think?
  Nobody never knew.
Somebody asked the Sergeant's Wife,
60 *An' she told 'em true!*
When you get to a man in the case,
  They're like as a row of pins –
For the Colonel's Lady an' Judy O'Grady
  Are sisters under their skins!

The Sergeant's Weddin'

'E was warned agin 'er –
  That's what made 'im look;
She was warned agin' 'im –
  That is why she took.
5 Wouldn't 'ear no reason,
  Went an' done it blind;
We know all about 'em,
  They've got all to find!

Cheer for the Sergeant's weddin' –
10   *Give 'em one cheer more!*
Grey gun-'orses in the lando,
   An' a rogue is married to, etc.

What's the use o' tellin'
   'Arf the lot she's been?
15   'E's a bloomin' robber,
   An' 'e keeps canteen.
'Ow did 'e get 'is buggy?
   Gawd, you needn't ask!
Made 'is forty gallon
20   Out of every cask!

Watch 'im, with 'is 'air cut,
   Count us filin' by –
Won't the Colonel praise 'is
   Pop-u-lar-i-ty!
25   We 'ave scores to settle –
   Scores for more than beer;
She's the girl to pay 'em –
   That is why we're 'ere!

See the Chaplain thinkin'?
30   See the women smile?
Twig the married winkin'
   As they take the aisle?
Keep your side-arms quiet,
   Dressin' by the Band.
35   Ho! You 'oly beggars,
   Cough be'ind your 'and!

Now it's done an' over,
   'Ear the organ squeak,
'Voice that breathed o'er Eden' –
40   Ain't she got the cheek!
White an' laylock ribbons,
   Think yourself so fine!
I'd pray Gawd to take yer
   'Fore I made yer mine!

45 Escort to the kerridge,
    Wish 'im luck, the brute!
Chuck the slippers after –
    (Pity 'taint a boot!)
Bowin' like a lady,
50   Blushin' like a lad –
'Oo would say to see 'em
    Both is rotten bad?

    Cheer for the Sergeant's weddin' –
      Give 'em one cheer more!
55   *Grey gun-'orses in the lando'*
      An' a rogue is married to, etc.

The Vampire

A fool there was and he made his prayer
(Even as you and I!)
To a rag and a bone and a hank of hair
(We called her the woman who did not care)
5 But the fool he called her his lady fair –
(Even as you and I!)

    Oh, the years we waste and the tears we waste
    And the work of our head and hand
    Belong to the woman who did not know
10   *(And now we know that she never could know)*
    And did not understand!

A fool there was and his goods he spent
(Even as you and I!)
Honour and faith and a sure intent
15 (And it wasn't the least what the lady meant)
But a fool must follow his natural bent
(Even as you and I!)

Oh, the toil we lost and the spoil we lost
And the excellent things we planned
20   *Belong to the woman who didn't know why*
     (And now we know that she never knew why)
     And did not understand!

The fool was stripped to his foolish hide
(Even as you and I!)
25   Which she might have seen when she threw him aside –
(But it isn't on record the lady tried)
So some of him lived but the most of him died –
(Even as you and I!)

And it isn't the shame, and it isn't the blame
30   *That stings like a white-hot brand –*
     It's coming to know that she never knew why
     (Seeing, at last, she could never know why)
     And never could understand!

Recessional

1897

God of our fathers, known of old,
   Lord of our far-flung battle-line,
Beneath whose awful Hand we hold
   Dominion over palm and pine –
5   Lord God of Hosts, be with us yet,
Lest we forget – lest we forget!

The tumult and the shouting dies;
   The Captains and the Kings depart:
Still stands Thine ancient sacrifice,
10   An humble and a contrite heart.
Lord God of Hosts, be with us yet,
Lest we forget – lest we forget!

Far-called, our navies melt away;
   On dune and headland sinks the fire:
15 Lo, all our pomp of yesterday
   Is one with Nineveh and Tyre!
Judge of the Nations, spare us yet,
Lest we forget – lest we forget!

If, drunk with sight of power, we loose
20   Wild tongues that have not Thee in awe,
Such boastings as the Gentiles use,
   Or lesser breeds without the Law –
Lord God of Hosts, be with us yet,
Lest we forget – lest we forget!

25 For heathen heart that puts her trust
   In reeking tube and iron shard,
All valiant dust that builds on dust,
   And guarding, calls not Thee to guard,
For frantic boast and foolish word –
30 Thy mercy on Thy People, Lord!

The White Man's Burden

1899

(THE UNITED STATES AND THE PHILIPPINE ISLANDS)

Take up the White Man's burden –
   Send forth the best ye breed –
Go, bind your sons to exile
   To serve your captives' need;
5 To wait in heavy harness
   On fluttered folk and wild –
Your new-caught, sullen peoples,
   Half devil and half child.

Take up the White Man's Burden –
10   In patience to abide,

To veil the threat of terror
    And check the show of pride;
By open speech and simple,
    An hundred times made plain,
15 To seek another's profit,
    And work another's gain.

Take up the White Man's burden –
    The savage wars of peace –
Fill full the mouth of Famine
20   And bid the sickness cease;
And when your goal is nearest
    The end for others sought,
Watch Sloth and heathen Folly
    Bring all your hope to nought.

25 Take up the White Man's burden –
    No tawdry rule of Kings,
But toil of serf and sweeper –
    The tale of common things.
The ports ye shall not enter,
30   The roads ye shall not tread,
Go make them with your living,
    And mark them with your dead!

Take up the White Man's burden –
    And reap his old reward:
35 The blame of those ye better,
    The hate of those ye guard –
The cry of hosts ye humour
    (Ah, slowly!) toward the light:–
'Why brought ye us from bondage,
40   Our loved Egyptian night?'

Take up the White Man's burden –
    Ye dare not stoop to less –
Nor call too loud on Freedom
    To cloak your weariness;
45 By all ye cry or whisper,

By all ye leave or do,
The silent, sullen peoples
    Shall weigh your Gods and you.

Take up the White Man's burden –
50   Have done with childish days –
The lightly proffered laurel,
    The easy, ungrudged praise.
Comes now, to search your manhood
    Through all the thankless years,
55 Cold-edged with dear-bought wisdom,
    The judgment of your peers!

Cruisers

As our mother the Frigate, bepainted and fine,
Made play for her bully the Ship of the Line;
So we, her bold daughters by iron and fire,
Accost and decoy to our masters' desire.

5   Now, pray you, consider what toils we endure,
Night-walking wet sea-lanes, a guard and a lure;
Since half of our trade is that same pretty sort
As mettlesome wenches do practise in port.

For this is our office – to spy and make room,
10 As hiding yet guiding the foe to their doom;
Surrounding, confounding, we bait and betray
And tempt them to battle the sea's width away.

The pot-bellied merchant foreboding no wrong
With headlight and sidelight he lieth along,
15 Till, lightless and lightfoot and lurking, leap we
To force him discover his business by sea.

And when we have wakened the lust of a foe,
To draw him by flight toward our bullies we go,
Till, 'ware of strange smoke stealing nearer, he flies
20 Ere our bullies close in for to make him good prize.

So, when we have spied on the path of their host,
One flieth to carry that word to the coast;
And, lest by false doublings they turn and go free,
One lieth behind them to follow and see.

25 Anon we return, being gathered again,
Across the sad valleys all drabbled with rain –
Across the grey ridges all crispèd and curled –
To join the long dance round the curve of the world.

The bitter salt spindrift, the sun-glare likewise,
30 The moon-track a-tremble, bewilders our eyes,
Where, linking and lifting, our sisters we hail
'Twixt wrench of cross-surges or plunge of head-gale.

As maidens awaiting the bride to come forth
Make play with light jestings and wit of no worth,
35 So, widdershins circling the bride-bed of death,
Each fleereth her neighbour and signeth and saith:–

'What see ye? Their signals, or levin afar?
What hear ye? God's thunder, or guns of our war?
What mark ye? Their smoke, or the cloud-rack outblown?
40 What chase ye? Their lights, or the Daystar low down?'

So, times past all number deceived by false shows,
Deceiving we cumber the road of our foes,
For this is our virtue: to track and betray;
Preparing great battles a sea's width away.

45 *Now peace is at end and our peoples take heart,*
For the laws are clean gone that restrainèd our art;
Up and down the near headlands and against the far wind
We are loosed (Oh, be swift!) to the work of our kind!

A School Song

'*Let us now praise famous men*' –
  Men of little showing –
For their work continueth,
And their work continueth,
5 *Broad and deep continueth,*
  Greater than their knowing!

Western wind and open surge
  Took us from our mothers,
Flung us on a naked shore
10 (Twelve bleak houses by the shore!
Seven summers by the shore!)
  'Mid two hundred brothers.

There we met with famous men
  Set in office o'er us;
15 And they beat on us with rods –
Faithfully with many rods –
Daily beat us on with rods,
  For the love they bore us!

Out of Egypt unto Troy –
20 Over Himalaya –
Far and sure our bands have gone –
Hy-Brasil or Babylon,
Islands of the Southern Run,
  And Cities of Cathaia!

25 *And* we all praise famous men –
  Ancients of the College;
For they taught us common sense –
Tried to teach us common sense –
Truth and God's Own Common Sense,
30 Which is more than knowledge!

Each degree of Latitude
  Strung about Creation

Seeth one or more of us
(Of one muster each of us),
35   Diligent in that he does,
    Keen in his vocation.

This we learned from famous men,
    Knowing not its uses,
When they showed, in daily work,
40   Man must finish off his work –
Right or wrong, his daily work –
    And without excuses.

Servants of the Staff and chain,
    Mine and fuse and grapnel –
45   Some, before the face of Kings,
Stand before the face of Kings;
Bearing gifts to divers Kings –
    Gifts of case and shrapnel.

This we learned from famous men
50   Teaching in our borders,
Who declarèd it was best,
Safest, easiest, and best –
Expeditious, wise, and best –
    To obey your orders.

55   Some beneath the further stars
    Bear the greater burden:
Set to serve the lands they rule,
(Save he serve no man may rule),
Serve and love the lands they rule;
60   Seeking praise nor guerdon.

This we learned from famous men,
    Knowing not we learned it.
Only, as the years went by –
Lonely, as the years went by –
65   Far from help as years went by,
    Plainer we discerned it.

Wherefore praise we famous men
  From whose bays we borrow –
They that put aside To-day –
70 All the joys of their To-day –
And with toil of their To-day
  Bought for us To-morrow!

Bless and praise we famous men –
  Men of little showing –
75 *For their work continueth,*
And their work continueth,
Broad and deep continueth,
  Great beyond their knowing!

The Absent-Minded Beggar

When you've shouted 'Rule Britannia,' when you've sung
    'God save the Queen,'
  When you've finished killing Kruger with your mouth,
Will you kindly drop a shilling in my little tambourine
  For a gentleman in khaki ordered South?
5 He's an absent-minded beggar, and his weaknesses are
        great –
  But we and Paul must take him as we find him –
He is out on active service, wiping something off a slate –
  And he's left a lot of little things behind him!
Duke's son – cook's son – son of a hundred Kings –
10   (Fifty thousand horse and foot going to Table Bay!)
Each of 'em doing his country's work
    (and who's to look after their things?)
Pass the hat for your credit's sake,
    and pay – pay – pay!

15 There are girls he married secret, asking no permission to,
  For he knew he wouldn't get it if he did.
There is gas and coals and vittles, and the house-rent
        falling due,

And it's more than rather likely there's a kid.
There are girls he walked with casual. They'll be sorry now
     he's gone,
20   For an absent-minded beggar they will find him,
But it ain't the time for sermons with the winter coming
     on,
    We must help the girl that Tommy's left behind him!
Cook's son – Duke's son – son of a belted Earl –
    Son of a Lambeth publican – it's all the same to-day!
25 Each of 'em doing his country's work
      (and who's to look after the girl?)
    Pass the hat for your credit's sake,
        and pay – pay – pay!

There are families by thousands, far too proud to beg or
     speak,
30   And they'll put their sticks and bedding up the spout,
And they'll live on half o' nothing, paid 'em punctual once
     a week,
    'Cause the man that earns the wage is ordered out.
He's an absent-minded beggar, but he heard his country
     call,
    And his Reg'ment didn't need to send to find him!
35 He chucked his job and joined it – so the job before us all
    Is to help the home that Tommy's left behind him!
Duke's job – cook's job – gardener, baronet, groom,
    Mews or palace or paper-shop, there's someone gone
     away!
Each of 'em doing his country's work
40   (and who's to look after the room?)
    Pass the hat for your credit's sake,
        and pay – pay – pay!

Let us manage so as, later, we can look him in the face,
    And tell him – what he'd very much prefer –
45 That, while he saved the Empire, his employer saved his
     place,
    And his mates (that's you and me) looked out for *her*.
He's an absent-minded beggar and he may forget it all,

But we do not want his kiddies to remind him
That we sent 'em to the workhouse while their daddy
      hammered Paul,
50   So we'll help the homes that Tommy left behind him!
Cook's home – Duke's home – home of a millionaire,
    (Fifty-thousand horse and foot going to Table Bay!)
Each of 'em doing his country's work
    (and what have you got to spare?)
55   Pass the hat for your credit's sake,
            and pay – pay – pay!

The Two-Sided Man

Much I owe to the Lands that grew –
More to the Lives that fed –
But most to Allah Who gave me two
Separate sides to my head.

5   Much I reflect on the Good and the True
In the Faiths beneath the sun,
But most upon Allah Who gave me two
Sides to my head, not one.

Wesley's following, Calvin's flock,
10   White or yellow or bronze,
Shaman, Ju-ju or Angekok,
Minister, Mukamuk, Bonze –

Here is a health, my brothers, to you,
However your prayers are said,
15   And praised be Allah Who gave me two
Separate sides to my head!

I would go without shirt or shoe,
Friend, tobacco or bread,
Sooner than lose for a minute the two
20   Separate sides of my head!

Bridge-Guard in the Karroo

'. . . and will supply details to guard the Blood River Bridge.'
District Orders: Lines of Communication – South African War

Sudden the desert changes,
    The raw glare softens and clings,
Till the aching Oudtshoorn ranges
    Stand up like the thrones of Kings –

5 Ramparts of slaughter and peril –
    Blazing, amazing, aglow –
'Twixt the sky-line's belting beryl
    And the wine-dark flats below.

Royal the pageant closes,
10   Lit by the last of the sun –
Opal and ash-of-roses,
    Cinnamon, umber, and dun.

The twilight swallows the thicket,
    The starlight reveals the ridge.
15 The whistle shrills to the picket –
    We are changing guard on the bridge.

(Few, forgotten and lonely,
    Where the empty metals shine –
No, not combatants – only
20   Details guarding the line.)

We slip through the broken panel
    Of fence by the ganger's shed;
We drop to the waterless channel
    And the lean track overhead;

25 We stumble on refuse of rations,
    The beef and the biscuit-tins;
We take our appointed stations,
    And the endless night begins.

We hear the Hottentot herders
30   As the sheep click past to the fold –
And the click of the restless girders
    As the steel contracts in the cold –

Voices of jackals calling
    And, loud in the hush between,
35 A morsel of dry earth falling
    From the flanks of the scarred ravine.

And the solemn firmament marches,
    And the hosts of heaven rise
Framed through the iron arches –
40   Banded and barred by the ties,

Till we feel the far track humming,
    And we see her headlight plain,
And we gather and wait her coming –
    The wonderful north-bound train.

45 (Few, forgotten and lonely,
    Where the white car-windows shine –
No, not combatants – only
    Details guarding the line.)

Quick, ere the gift escape us!
50   Out of the darkness we reach
For a handful of week-old papers
    And a mouthful of human speech.

And the monstrous heaven rejoices,
    And the earth allows again
55 Meetings, greetings, and voices
    Of women talking with men.

So we return to our places,
    As out on the bridge she rolls;
And the darkness covers our faces,
60   And the darkness re-enters our souls.

More than a little lonely
    Where the lessening tail-lights shine.
No – not combatants – only
    Details guarding the line!

The Lesson

(SOUTH AFRICAN WAR, 1899–1902)

Let us admit it fairly, as a business people should,
We have had no end of a lesson: it will do us no end of good.

Not on a single issue, or in one direction or twain,
But conclusively, comprehensively, and several times and
    again,
5 Were all our most holy illusions knocked higher than
    Gilderoy's kite.
We have had a jolly good lesson, and it serves us jolly well
    right!

This was not bestowèd us under the trees, nor yet in the
    shade of a tent,
But swingingly, over eleven degrees of a bare brown
    continent.
From Lamberts to Dalagoa Bay, and from Pietersburg to
    Sutherland,
10 Fell the phenomenal lesson we learned – with a fulness
    accorded no other land.

It was our fault, and our very great fault, and *not* the
    judgment of Heaven.
We made an Army in our image, on an island nine by
    seven,
Which faithfully mirrored its makers' ideals, equipment,
    and mental attitude –
And so we got our lesson: and we ought to accept it with
    gratitude.

15   We have spent two hundred million pounds to prove the
              fact once more,
      That horses are quicker than men afoot, since two and two
              make four;
      And horses have four legs, and men have two legs, and two
              into four goes twice,
      And nothing over except our lesson – and very cheap at the
              price.

      For remember (this our children shall know: we are too
              near for that knowledge)
20   Not our mere astonied camps, but Council and Creed and
              College –
      All the obese, unchallenged old things that stifle and overlie
              us –
      Have felt the effects of the lesson we got – an advantage no
              money could buy us!

      Then let us develop this marvellous asset which we alone
              command,
      And which, it may subsequently transpire, will be worth as
              much as the Rand.
25   Let us approach this pivotal fact in a humble yet hopeful
              mood –
      We have had no end of a lesson. It will do us no end of
              good!

      It was our fault, and our very great fault – and now we
              must turn it to use:
      We have forty million reasons for failure, but not a single
              excuse.
      So the more we work and the less we talk the better results
              we shall get.
30   We have had an Imperial lesson. It may make us an
              Empire yet!

The Islanders

No doubt but ye are the People – your throne is above the
                            King's.
Whoso speaks in your presence must say acceptable things:
Bowing the head in worship, bending the knee in fear –
Bringing the word well smoothen – such as a King should
                            hear.

5   Fenced by your careful fathers, ringed by your leaden seas,
Long did ye wake in quiet and long lie down at ease;
Till ye said of Strife, 'What is it?'; of the Sword, 'It is far
                            from our ken';
Till ye made a sport of your shrunken hosts and a toy of
                            your armèd men.
Ye stopped your ears to the warning – ye would neither
                            look nor heed –
10 Ye set your leisure before their toil and your lusts above
                            their need.
Because of your witless learning and your beasts of warren
                            and chase,
Ye grudged your sons to their service and your fields for
                            their camping-place.
Ye forced them glean in the highways the straw for the
                            bricks they brought;
Ye forced them follow in byways the craft that ye never
                            taught.
15 Ye hindered and hampered and crippled; ye thrust out of
                            sight and away
Those that would serve you for honour and those that
                            served you for pay.
Then were the judgments loosened; then was your shame
                            revealed,
At the hands of a little people, few but apt in the field.
Yet ye were saved by a remnant (and your land's long-
                            suffering star),
20 When your strong men cheered in their millions while your
                            striplings went to the war.

Sons of the sheltered city – unmade, unhandled, unmeet –
Ye pushed them raw to the battle as ye picked them raw
       from the street.
And what did ye look they should compass? Warcraft
       learned in a breath?
Knowledge unto occasion at the first far view of Death?
25 So! And ye train your horses and the dogs ye feed and
       prize?
How are the beasts more worthy than the souls, your
       sacrifice?
But ye said, 'Their valour shall show them'; but ye said,
       'The end is close.'
And ye sent them comfits and pictures to help them harry
       your foes:
And ye vaunted your fathomless power, and ye flaunted
       your iron pride,
30 Ere – ye fawned on the Younger Nations for the men who
       could shoot and ride!
Then ye returned to your trinkets; then ye contented your
       souls
With the flannelled fools at the wicket or the muddied oafs
       at the goals.
Given to strong delusion, wholly believing a lie,
Ye saw that the land lay fenceless, and ye let the months go
       by
35 Waiting some easy wonder, hoping some saving sign –
Idle – openly idle – in the lee of the forespent Line.
Idle – except for your boasting – and what is your boasting
       worth
If ye grudge a year of service to the lordliest life on earth?
Ancient, effortless, ordered, cycle on cycle set,
40 Life so long untroubled, that ye who inherit forget
It was not made with the mountains, it is not one with the
       deep.
Men, not gods, devised it. Men, not gods, must keep.
Men, not children, servants, nor kinsfolk called from afar,
But each man born in the Island broke to the matter of
       war.
45 Soberly and by custom taken and trained for the same,

Each man born in the Island entered at youth to the
       game –
As it were almost cricket, not to be mastered in haste,
But after trial and labour, by temperance, living chaste.
As it were almost cricket – as it were even your play,
50 Weighed and pondered and worshipped, and practised day
       and day.
So ye shall bide sure-guarded when the restless lightnings
       wake
In the womb of the blotting war-cloud, and the pallid
       nations quake.
So, at the haggard trumpets, instant your soul shall leap
Forthright, accoutred, accepting – alert from the wells of
       sleep.
55 So at the threat ye shall summon – so at the need ye shall
       send
Men, not children or servants, tempered and taught to the
       end;
Cleansed of servile panic, slow to dread or despise,
Humble because of knowledge, mighty by sacrifice . . .
But ye say, 'It will mar our comfort.' Ye say, 'It will
       minish our trade.'
60 Do ye wait for the spattered shrapnel ere ye learn how a
       gun is laid?
For the low, red glare to southward when the raided coast-
       towns burn?
(Light, ye shall have on that lesson, but little time to
       learn.)
Will ye pitch some white pavilion, and lustily even the
       odds,
With nets and hoops and mallets, with rackets and bats and
       rods?
65 Will the rabbit war with your foemen – the red deer horn
       them for hire?
Your kept cock-pheasant keep you? – he is master of many
       a shire.
Arid, aloof, incurious, unthinking, unthanking, gelt,
Will ye loose your schools to flout them till their brow-beat
       columns melt?

Will ye pray them, or preach them, or print them, or ballot
      them back from your shore?

70   Will your workmen issue a mandate to bid them strike no
      more?

Will ye rise and dethrone your rulers? (Because ye were
      idle both?

Pride by Insolence chastened? Indolence purged by Sloth?)

No doubt but ye are the People; who shall make you
      afraid?

Also your gods are many. No doubt but your gods shall
      aid.

75   Idols of greasy altars built for the body's ease;

Proud little brazen Baals and talking fetishes;

Teraphs of sept and party and wise wood – pavement
      gods –

These shall come down to the battle and snatch you from
      under the rods?

From the gusty, flickering gun-roll with viewless salvoes
      rent,

80   And the pitted hail of the bullets that tell not whence they
      were sent?

When ye are ringed as with iron, when ye are scourged as
      with whips,

When the meat is yet in your belly, and the boast is yet on
      your lips;

When ye go forth at morning and the noon beholds you broke,

Ere ye lie down at even, your remnant, under the yoke?

85   *No doubt but ye are the People – absolute, strong, and wise;*

Whatever your heart has desired ye have not withheld from
      your eyes.

On your own heads, in your own hands, the sin and the saving lies!

'The Camel's hump is an ugly lump'

The Camel's hump is an ugly lump
    Which well you may see at the Zoo;
But uglier yet is the Hump we get
    From having too little to do.

5   Kiddies and grown-ups too-oo-oo,
If we haven't enough to do-oo-oo,
        We get the Hump –
        Cameelious Hump –
The Hump that is black and blue!

10 We climb out of bed with frouzly head,
    And a snarly-yarly voice.
We shiver and scowl and we grunt and we growl
    At our bath and our boots and our toys;

And there ought to be a corner for me
15 (And I know there is one for you)
        When we get the Hump –
        Cameelious Hump –
The Hump that is black and blue!

The cure for this ill is not to sit still,
20   Or frowst with a book by the fire;
But to take a large hoe and a shovel also,
    And dig till you gently perspire;

And then you will find that the sun and the wind,
And the Djinn of the Garden too,
25   Have lifted the Hump –
        The horrible Hump –
The Hump that is black and blue!

I get it as well as you-oo-oo –
If I haven't enough to do-oo-oo!
30   We all get Hump –
        Cameelious Hump –
Kiddies and grown-ups too!

'I keep six honest serving-men'

I keep six honest serving-men
    (They taught me all I knew),
Their names are What and Why and When
    And How and Where and Who.
5   I send them over land and sea,
    I send them east and west;
But after they have worked for me,
    I give them all a rest.

I let them rest from nine till five,
10   For I am busy then,
As well as breakfast, lunch, and tea,
    For they are hungry men.
But different folk have different views.
    I know a person small –
15 She keeps ten million serving-men
    Who get no rest at all!

She sends 'em abroad on her own affairs,
    From the second she opens her eyes –
One million Hows, two million Wheres,
20   And seven million Whys!

'I've never sailed the Amazon'

I've never sailed the Amazon,
    I've never reached Brazil;
But the *Don* and *Magdalena*,
    They can go there when they will!

5   Yes, weekly from Southampton,
          Great steamers, white and gold,
          Go rolling down to Rio

(Roll down – roll down to Rio!)
And I'd like to roll to Rio
10   Some day before I'm old!

I've never seen a Jaguar,
    Nor yet an Armadill –
o dilloing in his armour,
    And I s'pose I never will,

15   Unless I go to Rio
        These wonders to behold –
        Roll down – roll down to Rio –
        Roll really down to Rio!
        Oh, I'd love to roll to Rio
20   Some day before I'm old!

'Pussy can sit by the fire and sing'

Pussy can sit by the fire and sing,
    Pussy can climb a tree,
Or play with a silly old cork and string
    To 'muse herself, not me.
5   But *I* like Binkie my dog, because
        He knows how to behave;
    So, Binkie's the same as the First Friend was,
        And I am the Man in the Cave!

Pussy will play Man Friday till
10   It's time to wet her paw
    And make her walk on the window-sill
        (For the footprint Crusoe saw);
    Then she fluffles her tail and mews,
        And scratches and won't attend.
15 But Binkie will play whatever I choose,
        And he is my true First Friend!

Pussy will rub my knees with her head
   Pretending she loves me hard;
But the very minute I go to my bed
20   Pussy runs out in the yard,
And there she stays till the morning-light;
   So I know it is only pretend.
But Binkie, he snores at my feet all night,
   And he is my Firstest Friend!

The Settler

(SOUTH AFRICAN WAR ENDED, MAY 1902)

Here, where my fresh-turned furrows run,
   And the deep soil glistens red,
I will repair the wrong that was done
   To the living and the dead.
5   Here, where the senseless bullet fell,
   And the barren shrapnel burst,
I will plant a tree, I will dig a well,
   Against the heat and the thirst.

Here, in a large and sunlit land,
10   Where no wrong bites to the bone,
I will lay my hand in my neighbour's hand,
   And together we will atone
For the set folly and the red breach
   And the black waste of it all;
15   Giving and taking counsel each
   Over the cattle-kraal.

Here will we join against our foes –
   The hailstroke and the storm,
And the red and rustling cloud that blows
20   The locust's mile-deep swarm.

Frost and murrain and floods let loose
    Shall launch us side by side
In the holy wars that have no truce
    'Twixt seed and harvest tide.

25 Earth, where we rode to slay or be slain,
    Our love shall redeem unto life.
We will gather and lead to her lips again
    The waters of ancient strife,
From the far and the fiercely guarded streams
30   And the pools where we lay in wait,
Till the corn cover our evil dreams
    And the young corn our hate.

And when we bring old fights to mind,
    We will not remember the sin –
35 If there be blood on his head of my kind,
    Or blood on my head of his kin –
For the ungrazed upland, the untilled lea
    Cry, and the fields forlorn:
'The dead must bury their dead, but ye –
40   Ye serve an host unborn.'

Bless then, Our God, the new-yoked plough
    And the good beasts that draw,
And the bread we eat in the sweat of our brow
    According to Thy Law.
45 After us cometh a multitude –
    Prosper the work of our hands,
That we may feed with our land's food
    The folk of all our lands!

Here, in the waves and the troughs of the plains,
50   Where the healing stillness lies,
And the vast, benignant sky restrains
    And the long days make wise –
Bless to our use the rain and the sun
    And the blind seed in its bed,
55 That we may repair the wrong that was done
    To the living and the dead!

'Before a midnight breaks in storm'

Before a midnight breaks in storm,
    Or herded sea in wrath,
Ye know what wavering gusts inform
    The greater tempest's path;
5   Till the loosed wind
        Drive all from mind,
Except Distress, which, so will prophets cry,
O'ercame them, houseless, from the unhinting sky.

Ere rivers league against the land
10   In piratry of flood,
Ye know what waters steal and stand
    Where seldom water stood.
        Yet who will note,
        Till fields afloat,
15 And washen carcass and the returning well,
Trumpet what these poor heralds strove to tell?

Ye know who use the Crystal Ball
    (To peer by stealth on Doom),
The Shade that, shaping first of all,
20   Prepares an empty room.
        Then doth It pass
        Like breath from glass,
But, on the extorted Vision bowed intent,
No man considers why It came or went.

25 Before the years reborn behold
    Themselves with stranger eye,
And the sport-making Gods of old,
    Like Samson slaying, die,
        Many shall hear
30   The all-pregnant sphere,
Bow to the birth and sweat, but – speech denied –
Sit dumb or – dealt in part – fall weak and wide.

Yet instant to fore-shadowed need
    The eternal balance swings;
35 That wingèd men the Fates may breed
    So soon as Fate hath wings.
      These shall possess
      Our littleness,
And in the imperial task (as worthy) lay
40 Up our lives' all to piece one giant Day.

The Second Voyage

We've sent our little Cupids all ashore –
    They were frightened, they were tired, they were cold.
Our sails of silk and purple go to store,
    And we've cut away our mast of beaten gold.
5   (Foul weather!)
Oh, 'tis hemp and singing pine for to stand against the
        brine,
    But Love he is our master as of old!

The sea has shorn our galleries away,
    The salt has soiled our gilding past remede;
10 Our paint is flaked and blistered by the spray,
    Our sides are half a fathom furred in weed.
        (Foul weather!)
And the Doves of Venus fled and the petrels came instead,
    But Love he was our master at our need!

15 'Was Youth would keep no vigil at the bow,
    'Was Pleasure at the helm too drunk to steer –
We've shipped three able quartermasters now.
    Men call them Custom, Reverence, and Fear.
        (Foul weather!)
20 They are old and scarred and plain, but we'll run no risk
        again
    From any Port o' Paphos mutineer!

We seek no more the tempest for delight,
    We skirt no more the indraught and the shoal –
We ask no more of any day or night
25   Than to come with least adventure to our goal.
          (Foul weather!)
What we find we needs must brook, but we do not go to
        look
    Nor tempt the Lord our God that saved us whole.

Yet, caring so, not overmuch we care
30   To brace and trim for every foolish blast –
If the squall be pleased to sweep us unaware,
    He may bellow off to leeward like the last.
          (Foul weather!)
We will blame it on the deep (for the watch must have
        their sleep),
35   And Love can come and wake us when 'tis past.

Oh, launch them down with music from the beach,
    Oh, warp them out with garlands from the quays –
Most resolute – a damsel unto each –
    New prows that seek the old Hesperides!
40   (Foul weather!)
Though we know their voyage is vain, yet we see our path
        again
    In the saffroned bridesails scenting all the seas!
          (Foul weather!)

The Broken Men

For things we never mention,
    For Art misunderstood –
For excellent intention
    That did not turn to good;
5   From ancient tales' renewing,
    From clouds we would not clear –
Beyond the Law's pursuing
    We fled, and settled here.

We took no tearful leaving,
10   We bade no long good-byes.
Men talked of crime and thieving,
      Men wrote of fraud and lies.
To save our injured feelings
      'Twas time and time to go –
15   Behind was dock and Dartmoor,
      Ahead lay Callao!

The widow and the orphan
      That pray for ten per cent,
They clapped their trailers on us
20   To spy the road we went.
They watched the foreign sailings
      (They scan the shipping still),
And that's your Christian people
      Returning good for ill!

25   God bless the thoughtful islands
      Where never warrants come;
God bless the just Republics
      That give a man a home,
That ask no foolish questions,
30   But set him on his feet;
And save his wife and daughters
      From the workhouse and the street!

On church and square and market
      The noonday silence falls;
35   You'll hear the drowsy mutter
      Of the fountain in our halls.
Asleep amid the yuccas
      The city takes her ease –
Till twilight brings the land-wind
40   To the clicking jalousies.

Day-long the diamond weather,
      The high, unaltered blue –
The smell of goats and incense
      And the mule-bells tinkling through.

45   Day-long the warder ocean
     That keeps us from our kin,
  And once a month our levee
     When the English mail comes in.

  You'll find us up and waiting
50   To treat you at the bar;
  You'll find us less exclusive
     Than the average English are.
  We'll meet you with a carriage,
     Too glad to show you round,
55   But – we do not lunch on steamers,
     For they are English ground.

  We sail o' nights to England
     And join our smiling Boards –
  Our wives go in with Viscounts
60   And our daughters dance with Lords,
  But behind our princely doings,
     And behind each coup we make,
  We feel there's Something Waiting,
     And – we meet It when we wake.

65   Ah, God! One sniff of England –
     To greet our flesh and blood –
  To hear the traffic slurring
     Once more through London mud!
  Our towns of wasted honour –
70   Our streets of lost delight!
  How stands the old 'Lord Warden?'
     Are Dover's cliffs still white?

Sussex

  God gave all men all earth to love,
     But, since our hearts are small,
  Ordained for each one spot should prove
     Belovèd over all;

5   That, as He watched Creation's birth
        So we, in godlike mood,
    May of our love create our earth
        And see that it is good.

    So one shall Baltic pines content,
10   As one some Surrey glade,
    Or one the palm-grove's droned lament
        Before Levuka's Trade.
    Each to his choice, and I rejoice
        The lot has fallen to me
15 In a fair ground – in a fair ground –
        Yea, Sussex by the sea!

    No tender-hearted garden crowns,
        No bosomed woods adorn
    Our blunt, bow-headed, whale-backed Downs,
20   But gnarled and writhen thorn –
    Bare slopes where chasing shadows skim,
        And, through the gaps revealed,
    Belt upon belt, the wooded, dim,
        Blue goodness of the Weald.

25 Clean of officious fence or hedge,
        Half-wild and wholly tame,
    The wise turf cloaks the white cliff-edge
        As when the Romans came.
    What sign of those that fought and died
30   At shift of sword and sword?
    The barrow and the camp abide,
        The sunlight and the sward.

    Here leaps ashore the full Sou'west
        All heavy-winged with brine,
35 Here lies above the folded crest
        The channel's leaden line;
    And here the sea-fogs lap and cling,
        And here, each warning each,
    The sheep-bells and the ship-bells ring
40   Along the hidden beach.

We have no waters to delight
    Our broad and brookless vales –
Only the dewpond on the height
    Unfed, that never fails –
45 Whereby no tattered herbage tells
    Which way the season flies –
Only our close-bit thyme that smells
    Like dawn in Paradise.

Here through the strong and shadeless days
50   The tinkling silence thrills;
Or little, lost, Down churches praise
    The Lord who made the hills:
But here the Old Gods guard their round,
    And, in her secret heart,
55 The heathen kingdom Wilfrid found
    Dreams, as she dwells, apart.

Though all the rest were all my share,
    With equal soul I'd see
Her nine-and-thirty sisters fair,
60   Yet none more fair than she.
Choose ye your need from Thames to Tweed,
    And I will choose instead
Such lands as lie 'twixt Rake and Rye,
    Black Down and Beachy Head.

65 I will go out against the sun
    Where the rolled scarp retires,
And the Long Man of Wilmington
    Looks naked towards the shires;
And east till doubling Rother crawls
70   To find the fickle tide,
By dry and sea-forgotten walls,
    Our ports of stranded pride.

I will go north about the shaws
    And the deep ghylls that breed

75 Huge oaks and old, the which we hold
        No more than 'Sussex weed';
    Or south where windy Piddinghoe's
        Begilded dolphin veers,
    And red beside wide-bankèd Ouse
80   Lie down our Sussex steers.

    So to the land our hearts we give
        Till the sure magic strike,
    And Memory, Use, and Love make live
        Us and our fields alike –
85 That deeper than our speech and thought,
        Beyond our reason's sway,
    Clay of the pit whence we were wrought
        Yearns to its fellow-clay.

    God gives all men all earth to love,
90   *But, since man's heart is small,*
    Ordains for each one spot shall prove
        Belovèd over all.
    Each to his choice, and I rejoice
        The lot has fallen to me
95 *In a fair ground – in a fair ground –*
        Yea, Sussex by the sea!

Dirge of Dead Sisters

(FOR THE NURSES WHO DIED IN THE
SOUTH AFRICAN WAR)

Who recalls the twilight and the rangèd tents in order
    (Violet peaks uplifted through the crystal evening air)
And the clink of iron teacups and the piteous, noble laughter,
    And the faces of the sisters with the dust upon their
                hair?

5   (Now and not hereafter, while the breath is in our nostrils,
       Now and not hereafter, ere the meaner years go by –
   Let us now remember many honourable women,
       Such as bade us turn again when we were like to die.)

   Who recalls the morning and the thunder through the
           foothills
10 (Tufts of fleecy shrapnel strung along the empty plains)
   And the sun-scarred Red-Cross coaches creeping guarded
           to the culvert,
       And the faces of the sisters looking gravely from the
           trains?

   (When the days were torment and the nights were clouded
           terror,
       When the Powers of Darkness had dominion on our
           soul –
15 When we fled consuming through the Seven Hells of
           Fever,
       These put out their hands to us and healed and made us
           whole.)

   Who recalls the midnight by the bridge's wrecked
           abutment
       (Autumn rain that rattled like a Maxim on the tin)
   And the lightning-dazzled levels and the streaming,
           straining wagons,
20   And the faces of the Sisters as they bore the wounded
           in?

   (Till the pain was merciful and stunned us into silence –
       When each nerve cried out on God that made the
           misused clay;
   When the Body triumphed and the last poor shame
           departed –
       These abode our agonies and wiped the sweat away.)

25 Who recalls the noontide and the funerals through the
market
(Blanket-hidden bodies, flagless, followed by the flies)
And the footsore firing-party, and the dust and stench and
staleness,
And the faces of the Sisters and the glory in their eyes?

(Bold behind the battle, in the open camp all-hallowed,
30 Patient, wise, and mirthful in the ringed and reeking
town,
These endured unresting till they rested from their
labours –
Little wasted bodies, ah, so light to lower down!)

Yet their graves are scattered and their names are clean
forgotten,
Earth shall not remember, but the Waiting Angel
knows
35 Them that died at Uitvlugt when the plague was on the
city –
Her that fell at Simon's Town in service on our foes.

Wherefore we they ransomed, while the breath is in our
nostrils,
Now and not hereafter – ere the meaner years go by –
Praise with love and worship many honourable women,
40 *Those that gave their lives for us when we were like*
to die!

Chant-Pagan

(ENGLISH IRREGULAR, DISCHARGED)

Me that 'ave been what I've been –
Me that 'ave gone where I've gone –
Me that 'ave seen what I've seen –
'Ow can I ever take on
5 With awful old England again,

An' 'ouses both sides of the street,
An' 'edges two sides of the lane,
An' the parson an' gentry between,
An' touchin' my 'at when we meet –
10   Me that 'ave been what I've been?

Me that 'ave watched 'arf a world
'Eave up all shiny with dew,
Kopje on kop to the sun,
An' as soon as the mist let 'em through
15   Our 'elios winkin' like fun –
Three sides of a ninety-mile square,
Over valleys as big as a shire –
'*Are ye there? Are ye there? Are ye there?*'
An' then the blind drum of our fire . . .
20   An' I'm rollin' 'is lawns for the Squire,

                                        Me!

Me that 'ave rode through the dark
Forty miles, often, on end,
Along the Ma'ollisberg Range,
25   With only the stars for my mark
An' only the night for my friend,
An' things runnin' off as you pass,
An' things jumpin' up in the grass,
An' the silence, the shine an' the size
30   Of the 'igh, unexpressible skies –
I am takin' some letters almost
As much as a mile to the post,
An' 'mind you come back with the change!'

                                        Me!

35   Me that saw Barberton took
When we dropped through the clouds on their 'ead,
An' they 'ove the guns over and fled –
Me that was through Di'mond 'Ill,
An' Pieters an' Springs an' Belfast –
40   From Dundee to Vereeniging all –
Me that stuck out to the last
(An' five bloomin' bars on my chest) –

I am doin' my Sunday-school best,
By the 'elp of the Squire an' 'is wife
45 (Not to mention the 'ousemaid an' cook),
To come in an' 'ands up an' be still,
An' honestly work for my bread,
My livin' in that state of life
To which it shall please Gawd to call
50   Me!

Me that 'ave followed my trade
In the place where the Lightnin's are made;
'Twixt the Rains an' the Sun an' the Moon –
Me that lay down an' got up
55 Three years with the sky for my roof –
That 'ave ridden my 'unger an' thirst
Six thousand raw mile on the hoof,
With the Vaal an' the Orange for cup,
An' the Brandwater Basin for dish, –
60 Oh! it's 'ard to be'ave as they wish
(Too 'ard, an' a little too soon),
I'll 'ave to think over it first –

                                            Me!

I will arise an' get 'ence –
65 I will trek South an' make sure
If it's only my fancy or not
That the sunshine of England is pale,
An' the breezes of England are stale,
An' there's somethin' gone small with the lot.
70 For *I* know of a sun an' a wind,
An' some plains an' a mountain be'ind,
An' some graves by a barb-wire fence,
An' a Dutchman I've fought 'oo might give
Me a job were I ever inclined
75 To look in an' offsaddle an' live
Where there's neither a road nor a tree –
But only my Maker an' me,
An' I think it will kill me or cure,
So I think I will go there an' see.
80   Me!

Lichtenberg

(NEW SOUTH WALES CONTINGENT)

Smells are surer than sounds or sights
    To make your heart-strings crack –
They start those awful voices o' nights
    That whisper, 'Old man, come back!'
5 That must be why the big things pass
    And the little things remain,
Like the smell of the wattle by Lichtenberg,
    Riding in, in the rain.

There was some silly fire on the flank
10   And the small wet drizzling down –
There were the sold-out shops and the bank
    And the wet, wide-open town;
And we were doing escort-duty
    To somebody's baggage-train,
15 And I smelt wattle by Lichtenberg –
    Riding in, in the rain.

It was all Australia to me –
    All I had found or missed:
Every face I was crazy to see,
20   And every woman I'd kissed;
All that I shouldn't ha' done, God knows!
    (As He knows I'll do it again),
That smell of the wattle round Lichtenberg,
    Riding in, in the rain!

25 And I saw Sydney the same as ever,
    The picnics and brass bands;
And my little homestead on Hunter River
    And my new vines joining hands.
It all came over me in one act
30   Quick as a shot through the brain –
With the smell of the wattle round Lichtenberg,
    Riding in, in the rain.

I have forgotten a hundred fights,
    But one I shall not forget –
35 With the raindrops bunging up my sights
    And my eyes bunged up with wet;
And through the crack and the stink of the cordite,
    (Ah, Christ! My country again!)
The smell of the wattle by Lichtenberg,
40   Riding in, in the rain!

Stellenbosch

(COMPOSITE COLUMNS)

The General 'eard the firin' on the flank,
    An' 'e sent a mounted man to bring 'im back
The silly, pushin' person's name an' rank
    'Oo'd dared to answer Brother Boer's attack:
5 For there might 'ave been a serious engagement,
    An' 'e might 'ave wasted 'alf a dozen men;
So 'e ordered 'im to stop 'is operations round the kopjes,
    An' 'e told 'im off before the Staff at ten!

        An' it all goes into the laundry,
10   But it never comes out in the wash,
        'Ow we're sugared about by the old men
        ('Eavy-sterned amateur old men!)
        That 'amper an' 'inder an' scold men
        For fear o' Stellenbosch!

15 The General 'ad 'produced a great effect,'
    The General 'ad the country cleared – almost;
The General ''ad no reason to expect,'
    An' the Boers 'ad us bloomin' well on toast!
For we might 'ave crossed the drift before the twilight,
20   Instead o' sittin' down an' takin' root;
But we was not allowed, so the Boojers scooped the crowd,
    To the last survivin' bandolier an' boot.

The General saw the farm'ouse in 'is rear,
 With its stoep so nicely shaded from the sun;
25 Sez 'e, 'I'll pitch my tabernacle 'ere,'
  An' 'e kept us muckin' round till 'e 'ad done.
For 'e might 'ave caught the confluent pneumonia
 From sleepin' in his gaiters in the dew;
So 'e took a book an' dozed while the other columns
   closed,
30 An' De Wet's commando out an' trickled through!

The General saw the mountain-range ahead,
 With their 'elios showin' saucy on the 'eight,
So 'e 'eld us to the level ground instead,
 An' telegraphed the Boojers wouldn't fight.
35 For 'e might 'ave gone an' sprayed 'em with a pompom,
  Or 'e might 'ave slung a squadron out to see –
But 'e wasn't takin' chances in them 'igh and 'ostile
   kranzes –
He was markin' time to earn a K.C.B.

The General got 'is decorations thick
40 (The men that backed 'is lies could not complain),
The Staff 'ad D.S.O.'s till we was sick,
 An' the soldier – 'ad the work to do again!
For 'e might 'ave known the District was an 'otbed,
 Instead of 'andin' over, upside-down,
45 To a man 'oo 'ad to fight 'alf a year to put it right,
  While the General sat an' slandered 'im in town!

  An' it all went into the laundry,
  But it never came out in the wash.
  We were sugared about by the old men
50 (Panicky, perishin' old men)
  That 'amper an' 'inder an' scold men
  For fear o' Stellenbosch!

Harp Song of the Dane Women

What is a woman that you forsake her,
And the hearth-fire and the home-acre,
To go with the old grey Widow-maker?

She has no house to lay a guest in –
5 But one chill bed for all to rest in,
That the pale suns and the stray bergs nest in.

She has no strong white arms to fold you,
But the ten-times-fingering weed to hold you –
Out on the rocks where the tide has rolled you.

10 Yet, when the signs of summer thicken,
And the ice breaks, and the birch-buds quicken,
Yearly you turn from our side, and sicken –

Sicken again for the shouts and the slaughters, –
And steal away to the lapping waters,
15 And look at your ship in her winter-quarters.

You forget our mirth, and talk at the tables,
The kine in the shed and the horse in the stables –
To pitch her sides and go over her cables.

Then you drive out where the storm-clouds swallow,
20 And the sound of your oar-blades, falling hollow,
Is all we have left through the months to follow.

Ah, what is Woman that you forsake her,
And the hearth-fire and the home-acre,
To go with the old grey Widow-maker?

'Rimini'

(MARCHING SONG OF A ROMAN LEGION OF
THE LATER EMPIRE)

When I left Rome for Lalage's sake,
By the Legions' Road to Rimini,
She vowed her heart was mine to take
With me and my shield to Rimini –
5 (Till the Eagles flew from Rimini –)
And I've tramped Britain, and I've tramped Gaul,
And the Pontic shore where the snow-flakes fall
As white as the neck of Lalage –
(As cold as the heart of Lalage!)
10 And I've lost Britain, and I've lost Gaul,
And I've lost Rome and, worst of all,
I've lost Lalage!

When you go by the Via Aurelia,
As thousands have travelled before,
15 Remember the Luck of the Soldier
Who never saw Rome any more!
Oh, dear was the sweetheart that kissed him,
And dear was the mother that bore;
But his shield was picked up in the heather,
20 And he never saw Rome any more!

And *he* left Rome, etc.

When you go by the Via Aurelia
That runs from the City to Gaul,
Remember the Luck of the Soldier
25 Who rose to be master of all!
He carried the sword and the buckler,
He mounted his guard on the Wall,
Till the Legions elected him Caesar,
And he rose to be master of all!

30 And *he* left Rome, etc.

It's twenty-five marches to Narbo,
It's forty-five more up the Rhone,
And the end may be death in the heather
Or life on an Emperor's throne.
35 But whether the Eagles obey us,
Or we go to the Ravens – alone,
I'd sooner be Lalage's lover
Than sit on an Emperor's throne!

We've *all* left Rome for Lalage's sake, etc.

Prophets at Home

Prophets have honour all over the Earth,
    Except in the village where they were born,
Where such as knew them boys from birth
    Nature-ally hold 'em in scorn.

5   When Prophets are naughty and young and vain,
    They make a won'erful grievance of it;
(You can see by their writings how they complain),
    But Oh, 'tis won'erful good for the Prophet!

There's nothing Nineveh Town can give
10   (Nor being swallowed by whales between),
Makes up for the place where a man's folk live,
    Which don't care nothing what he has been.
He might ha' been that, or he might ha' been this,
But they love and they hate him for what he is.

A Smuggler's Song

If you wake at midnight, and hear a horse's feet,
Don't go drawing back the blind, or looking in the street,
Them that asks no questions isn't told a lie.
Watch the wall, my darling, while the Gentlemen go by!

5   Five-and-twenty ponies
          Trotting through the dark –
          Brandy for the parson,
          'Baccy for the Clerk;
          Laces for a lady, letters for a spy,
10   And watch the wall, my darling, while the Gentlemen go
              by!

Running round the woodlump if you chance to find
Little barrels, roped and tarred, all full of brandy-wine,
Don't you shout to come and look, nor use 'em for your
            play.
Put the brishwood back again – and they'll be gone next
            day!

15   If you see the stable-door setting open wide;
     If you see a tired horse lying down inside;
     If your mother mends a coat cut about and tore;
     If the lining's wet and warm – don't you ask no more!

If you meet King George's men, dressed in blue and
            red,
20   You be careful what you say, and mindful what is
            said.
If they call you 'pretty maid,' and chuck you 'neath the
            chin,
Don't tell where no one is, nor yet where no one's been!

Knocks and footsteps round the house – whistles after
            dark –
You've no call for running out till the house-dogs bark.
25   Trusty's here, and Pincher's here, and see how dumb they
            lie –
They don't fret to follow when the Gentlemen go by!

If you do as you've been told, 'likely there's a chance,
You'll be give a dainty doll, all the way from France,
With a cap of Valenciennes, and a velvet hood –
30   A present from the Gentlemen, along o' being good!

Five-and-twenty ponies
Trotting through the dark –
Brandy for the Parson,
'Baccy for the Clerk.
35   Them that asks no questions isn't told a lie –
Watch the wall, my darling, while the Gentlemen go by!

The Sons of Martha

The Sons of Mary seldom bother, for they have inherited
          that good part;
But the Sons of Martha favour their Mother of the careful
          soul and the troubled heart.
And because she lost her temper once, and because she was
          rude to the Lord her Guest,
Her Sons must wait upon Mary's Sons, world without end,
          reprieve, or rest.

5   It is their care in all the ages to take the buffet and cushion
          the shock.
It is their care that the gear engages; it is their care that the
          switches lock.
It is their care that the wheels run truly; it is their care to
          embark and entrain,
Tally, transport, and deliver duly the Sons of Mary by
          land and main.

They say to mountains, 'Be ye removèd.' They say to the
          lesser floods, 'Be dry.'
10   Under their rods are the rocks reprovèd – they are not
          afraid of that which is high.
Then do the hill-tops shake to the summit – then is the
          bed of the deep laid bare,
That the Sons of Mary may overcome it, pleasantly sleeping
          and unaware.

They finger Death at their gloves' end where they piece
and repiece the living wires.

He rears against the gates they tend: they feed him hungry
behind their fires.

15   Early at dawn, ere men see clear, they stumble into his
terrible stall,

And hale him forth like a haltered steer, and goad and turn
him till evenfall.

To these from birth is Belief forbidden; from these till
death is Relief afar.

They are concerned with matters hidden – under the
earth-line their altars are –

The secret fountains to follow up, waters withdrawn to
restore to the mouth,

20   And gather the floods as in a cup, and pour them again at a
city's drouth.

They do not preach that their God will rouse them a little
before the nuts work loose.

They do not teach that His Pity allows them to drop their
job when they dam'-well choose.

As in the thronged and the lighted ways, so in the dark and
the desert they stand,

Wary and watchful all their days that their brethren's days
may be long in the land.

25   Raise ye the stone or cleave the wood to make a path more
fair or flat –

Lo, it is black already with blood some Son of Martha
spilled for that!

Not as a ladder from earth to Heaven, not as a witness to
any creed,

But simple service simply given to his own kind in their
common need.

And the Sons of Mary smile and are blessèd – they know
the Angels are on their side.

30   They know in them is the Grace confessèd, and for them
are the Mercies multiplied.

They sit at the Feet – they hear the Word – they see how
      truly the Promise runs.
They have cast their burden upon the Lord, and – the
      Lord He lays it on Martha's Sons!

A Song of Travel

Where's the lamp that Hero lit
    Once to call Leander home?
Equal Time hath shovelled it
    'Neath the wrack of Greece and Rome.
5 Neither wait we any more
That worn sail which Argo bore.

Dust and dust of ashes close
    All the Vestal Virgins' care;
And the oldest altar shows
10   But an older darkness there.
Age-encamped Oblivion
Tenteth every light that shone.

Yet shall we, for Suns that die,
    Wall our wanderings from desire?
15 Or, because the Moon is high,
    Scorn to use a nearer fire?
Lest some envious Pharaoh stir,
Make our lives our sepulchre?

Nay! Though Time with petty Fate
20   Prison us and Emperors,
By our Arts do we create
    That which Time himself devours –
Such machines as well may run
'Gainst the Horses of the Sun.

25 When we would a new abode,
    Space, our tyrant King no more,
Lays the long lance of the road
    At our feet and flees before,
Breathless, ere we overwhelm,
30 To submit a further realm!

'The Power of the Dog'

There is sorrow enough in the natural way
From men and women to fill our day;
And when we are certain of sorrow in store,
Why do we always arrange for more?
5 *Brothers and Sisters, I bid you beware*
Of giving your heart to a dog to tear.

Buy a pup and your money will buy
Love unflinching that cannot lie –
Perfect passion and worship fed
10 By a kick in the ribs or a pat on the head.
Nevertheless it is hardly fair
To risk your heart for a dog to tear.

When the fourteen years which Nature permits
Are closing in asthma, or tumour, or fits,
15 And the vet's unspoken prescription runs
To lethal chambers or loaded guns,
Then you will find – it's your own affair –
But . . . you've given your heart to a dog to tear.

When the body that lived at your single will,
20 With its whimper of welcome, is stilled (how still!)
When the spirit that answered your every mood
Is gone – wherever it goes – for good,
You will discover how much you care,
And will give your heart to a dog to tear.

25 We've sorrow enough in the natural way,
   When it comes to burying Christian clay.
   Our loves are not given, but only lent,
   At compound interest of cent per cent.

   Though it is not always the case, I believe,
30 That the longer we've kept 'em, the more do we grieve:
   For, when debts are payable, right or wrong,
   A short-time loan is as bad as a long –
   So why in–Heaven (before we are there)
   Should we give our hearts to a dog to tear?

The Puzzler

The Celt in all his variants from Builth to Ballyhoo,
His mental processes are plain – one knows what he will
        do,
And can logically predicate his finish by his start;
But the English – ah, the English! – they are quite a race
        apart.

5 Their psychology is bovine, their outlook crude and raw.
They abandon vital matters to be tickled with a straw;
But the straw that they were tickled with – the chaff that
        they were fed with –
They convert into a weaver's beam to break their foeman's
        head with.

For undemocratic reasons and for motives not of State,
10 They arrive at their conclusion – largely inarticulate.
Being void of self-expression they confide their views to
        none;
But sometimes in a smoking-room, one learns why things
        were done.

Yes, sometimes in a smoking-room, through clouds of 'Ers'
        and 'Ums,'
Obliquely and by inference, illumination comes,

15 On some step that they have taken, or some action they
approve –
Embellished with the *argot* of the Upper Fourth Remove.

In telegraphic sentences, half nodded to their friends,
They hint a matter's inwardness – and there the matter
ends.
And while the Celt is talking from Valencia to Kirkwall,
20 The English – ah, the English! – don't say anything at
all.

The Rabbi's Song

II SAMUEL 14:14

If Thought can reach to Heaven,
    On Heaven let it dwell,
For fear thy Thought be given
    Like power to reach to Hell;
5 For fear the desolation
    And darkness of thy mind
Perplex an habitation
    Which thou hast left behind.

Let nothing linger after –
10   No whimpering ghost remain,
In wall, or beam, or rafter,
    Of any hate or pain.
Cleanse and call home thy spirit,
    Deny her leave to cast,
15 On aught thy heirs inherit,
    The shadow of her past.

For think, in all thy sadness,
    What road our griefs may take;
Whose brain reflect our madness,
20   Or whom our terrors shake:

For think, lest any languish
    By cause of thy distress –
The arrows of our anguish
    Fly farther than we guess.

25   Our lives, our tears, as water,
      Are spilled upon the ground:
God giveth no man quarter,
      Yet God a means hath found –
Though Faith and Hope have vanished,
30   And even Love grows dim –
A means whereby His banished
      Be not expelled from Him!

A Charm

Take of English earth as much
As either hand may rightly clutch.
In the taking of it breathe
Prayer for all who lie beneath.
5   Not the great nor well-bespoke,
But the mere uncounted folk
Of whose life and death is none
Report or lamentation.
    Lay that earth upon thy heart,
10   And thy sickness shall depart!

It shall sweeten and make whole
Fevered breath and festered soul.
It shall mightily restrain
Over-busied hand and brain.
15   It shall ease thy mortal strife
'Gainst the immortal woe of life,
Till thyself, restored, shall prove
By what grace the Heavens do move.

Take of English flowers these –
20   Spring's full-facèd primroses,
     Summer's wild wide-hearted rose,
     Autumn's wall-flower of the close,
     And, thy darkness to illume,
     Winter's bee-thronged ivy-bloom.
25   Seek and serve them where they bide
     From Candlemas to Christmas-tide,
         For these simples, used aright,
         Can restore a failing sight.

     These shall cleanse and purify
30   Webbed and inward-turning eye;
     These shall show thee treasure hid,
     Thy familiar fields amid;
     At thy threshold, on thy hearth,
     Or about thy daily path;
35   And reveal (which is thy need)
     Every man a King indeed!

Cold Iron

Gold is for the mistress – silver for the maid –
Copper for the craftsman cunning at his trade.
'Good!' said the Baron, sitting in his hall,
'But Iron – Cold Iron – is master of them all.'

5   So he made rebellion 'gainst the King his liege,
     Camped before his citadel and summoned it to siege.
     'Nay!' said the cannoneer on the castle wall,
     'But Iron – Cold Iron – shall be master of you all!'

     Woe for the Baron and his knights so strong,
10   When the cruel cannon-balls laid 'em all along;
     He was taken prisoner, he was cast in thrall,
     And Iron – Cold Iron – was master of it all!

Yet his King spake kindly (ah, how kind a Lord!)
'What if I release thee now and give thee back thy sword?'
15 'Nay!' said the Baron, 'mock not at my fall,
For Iron – Cold Iron – is master of men all.'

Tears are for the craven, prayers are for the clown –
Halters for the silly neck that cannot keep a crown.
'As my loss is grievous, so my hope is small,
20 For Iron – Cold Iron – must be master of men all!'

Yet his King made answer (few such Kings there be!)
'Here is Bread and here is Wine – sit and sup with me.
Eat and drink in Mary's Name, the whiles I do recall
How Iron – Cold Iron – can be master of men all!'

25 He took the Wine and blessed it. He blessed and brake the
Bread.
With His own Hands He served Them, and presently He
said:
'See! These Hands they pierced with nails, outside My city
wall,
Show Iron – Cold Iron – to be master of men all!

Wounds are for the desperate, blows are for the strong –
30 Balm and oil for weary hearts all cut and bruised with
wrong.
I forgive thy treason – I redeem thy fall –
For Iron – Cold Iron – must be master of men all!'

Crowns are for the valiant – sceptres for the bold!
Thrones and powers for mighty men who dare to take and
hold!
35 'Nay!' said the Baron, kneeling in his hall,
'But Iron – Cold Iron – is master of men all!
Iron out of Calvary is master of men all!'

The Looking-Glass

(A COUNTRY DANCE)

Queen Bess was Harry's daughter. (Stand forward partners
    all!)
In ruff and stomacher and gown
She danced King Philip down-a-down,
And left her shoe to show 'twas true –
5   *(The very tune I'm playing you)*
In Norgem at Brickwall!

The Queen was in her chamber, and she was middling old.
Her petticoat was satin, and her stomacher was gold.
Backwards and forwards and sideways did she pass,
10 Making up her mind to face the cruel looking-glass.
The cruel looking-glass that will never show a lass
As comely or as kindly or as young as what she was!

Queen Bess was Harry's daughter. (Now hand your partners
    all!)

The Queen was in her chamber, a-combing of her hair.
15 There came Queen Mary's spirit and It stood behind her
        chair,
Singing, 'Backwards and forwards and sideways may you
        pass,
But I will stand behind you till you face the looking-glass.
The cruel looking-glass that will never show a lass
As lovely or unlucky or as lonely as I was!'

20 *Queen Bess was Harry's daughter. (Now turn your partners*
    all!)

The Queen was in her chamber, a-weeping very sore.
There came Lord Leicester's spirit and It scratched upon
        the door,
Singing, 'Backwards and forwards and sideways may you
        pass,

But I will walk beside you till you face the looking-glass.
25 The cruel looking-glass that will never show a lass,
As hard and unforgiving or as wicked as you was!'

Queen Bess was Harry's daughter. (Now kiss your partners
all!)

The Queen was in her chamber, her sins were on her head.
She looked the spirits up and down and statelily she said: —
30 'Backwards and forwards and sideways though I've been,
Yet I am Harry's daughter and I am England's Queen!'
And she faced the looking-glass (and whatever else there
was)
And she saw her day was over and she saw her beauty pass
In the cruel looking-glass, that can always hurt a lass
35 More hard than any ghost there is or any man there was!

The Way through the Woods

They shut the road through the woods
Seventy years ago.
Weather and rain have undone it again,
And now you would never know
5 There was once a road through the woods
Before they planted the trees.
It is underneath the coppice and heath
And the thin anemones.
Only the keeper sees
10 That, where the ring-dove broods,
And the badgers roll at ease,
There was once a road through the woods.

Yet, if you enter the woods
Of a summer evening late,
15 When the night-air cools on the trout-ringed pools
Where the otter whistles his mate,
(They fear not men in the woods,

Because they see so few.)
You will hear the beat of a horse's feet,
20   And the swish of a skirt in the dew,
Steadily cantering through
The misty solitudes,
As though they perfectly knew
The old lost road through the woods . . .
25   But there is no road through the woods!

If –

If you can keep your head when all about you
    Are losing theirs and blaming it on you,
If you can trust yourself when all men doubt you,
    But make allowance for their doubting too;
5   If you can wait and not be tired by waiting,
    Or being lied about, don't deal in lies,
Or being hated, don't give way to hating,
    And yet don't look too good, nor talk too wise:

If you can dream – and not make dreams your master;
10   If you can think – and not make thoughts your aim;
If you can meet with Triumph and Disaster
    And treat those two impostors just the same;
If you can bear to hear the truth you've spoken
    Twisted by knaves to make a trap for fools,
15   Or watch the things you gave your life to, broken,
    And stoop and build 'em up with worn-out tools:

If you can make one heap of all your winnings
    And risk it on one turn of pitch-and-toss,
And lose, and start again at your beginnings
20   And never breathe a word about your loss;
If you can force your heart and nerve and sinew
    To serve your turn long after they are gone,
And so hold on when there is nothing in you
    Except the Will which says to them: 'Hold on!'

25 If you can talk with crowds and keep your virtue,
        Or walk with Kings – nor lose the common touch,
    If neither foes nor loving friends can hurt you,
        If all men count with you, but none too much;
    If you can fill the unforgiving minute
30   With sixty seconds' worth of distance run,
    Yours is the Earth and everything that's in it,
        And – which is more – you'll be a Man, my son!

'Poor Honest Men'

    Your jar of Virginny
    Will cost you a guinea,
    Which you reckon too much by five shilling or ten;
    But light your churchwarden
5   And judge it accordin',
    When I've told you the troubles of poor honest men.

    From the Capes of the Delaware,
    As you are well aware,
    We sail with tobacco for England – but then,
10 Our own British cruisers,
    They watch us come through, sirs,
    And they press half a score of us poor honest men!

    Or if by quick sailing
    (Thick weather prevailing)
15 We leave them behind (as we do now and then)
    We are sure of a gun from
    Each frigate we run from,
    Which is often destruction to poor honest men!

    Broadsides the Atlantic
20 We tumble short-handed,
    With shot-holes to plug and new canvas to bend;
    And off the Azores,
    Dutch, Dons and Monsieurs
    Are waiting to terrify poor honest men.

25   Napoleon's embargo
Is laid on all cargo
Which comfort or aid to King George may intend;
And since roll, twist and leaf,
Of all comforts is chief,
30   They try for to steal it from poor honest men!

With no heart for fight,
We take refuge in flight,
But fire as we run, our retreat to defend,
Until our stern-chasers
35   Cut up her fore-braces,
And she flies off the wind from us poor honest men!

Twix' the Forties and Fifties,
South-eastward the drift is,
And so, when we think we are making Land's End,
40   Alas, it is Ushant
With half the King's Navy,
Blockading French ports against poor honest men!

But they may not quit station
(Which is our salvation)
45   So swiftly we stand to the Nor'ard again;
And finding the tail of
A homeward-bound convoy,
We slip past the Scillies like poor honest men.

Twix' the Lizard and Dover,
50   We hand our stuff over,
Though I may not inform how we do it, nor when.
But a light on each quarter,
Low down on the water,
Is well understanded by poor honest men.

55   Even then we have dangers,
From meddlesome strangers,
Who spy on our business and are not content

To take a smooth answer,
Except with a handspike . . .
60 And they say they are murdered by poor honest men!

To be drowned or be shot
Is our natural lot,
Why should we, moreover, be hanged in the end –
After all our great pains
65 For to dangle in chains
As though we were smugglers, not poor honest men?

'Our Fathers of Old'

Excellent herbs had our fathers of old –
    Excellent herbs to ease their pain –
Alexanders and Marigold,
    Eyebright, Orris, and Elecampane –
5 Basil, Rocket, Valerian, Rue,
    (Almost singing themselves they run)
Vervain, Dittany, Call-me-to-you –
    Cowslip, Melilot, Rose of the Sun.
        Anything green that grew out of the mould
10   Was an excellent herb to our fathers of old.

Wonderful tales had our fathers of old,
    Wonderful tales of the herbs and the stars –
The Sun was Lord of the Marigold,
    Basil and Rocket belonged to Mars.
15 Pat as a sum in division it goes –
    (Every herb had a planet bespoke) –
Who but Venus should govern the Rose?
    Who but Jupiter own the Oak?
        Simply and gravely the facts are told
20   In the wonderful books of our fathers of old.

Wonderful little, when all is said,
    Wonderful little our fathers knew.
Half their remedies cured you dead –
    Most of their teaching was quite untrue –
25 'Look at the stars when a patient is ill
    (Dirt has nothing to do with disease),
Bleed and blister as much as you will,
    Blister and bleed him as oft as you please.'
      Whence enormous and manifold
30   Errors were made by our fathers of old.

Yet when the sickness was sore in the land,
    And neither planets nor herbs assuaged,
They took their lives in their lancet-hand
    And, oh, what a wonderful war they waged!
35 Yes, when the crosses were chalked on the door –
    (Yes, when the terrible dead-cart rolled!)
Excellent courage our fathers bore –
    Excellent heart had our fathers of old.
      None too learned, but nobly bold
40   Into the fight went our fathers of old.

If it be certain, as Galen says –
    And sage Hippocrates holds as much –
'That those afflicted by doubts and dismays
    Are mightily helped by a dead man's touch,'
45 Then, be good to us, stars above!
    Then, be good to us, herbs below!
We are afflicted by what we can prove,
    We are distracted by what we know.
      So-ah, so!
50   Down from your heaven or up from your mould,
      Send us the hearts of our fathers of old!

The Declaration of London

29 JUNE, 1911

On the reassembling of Parliament after the Coronation, the Government have no intention of allowing their followers to vote according to their convictions on the Declaration of London, but insist on a strictly party vote.

Daily Papers

We were all one heart and one race
    When the Abbey trumpets blew.
For a moment's breathing-space
    We had forgotten you.
5 Now you return to your honoured place
    Panting to shame us anew.

We have walked with the Ages dead –
    With our Past alive and ablaze:
And you bid us pawn our honour for bread,
10   This day of all the days!
And you cannot wait till our guests are sped,
    Or last week's wreath decays?

The light is still in our eyes
    Of Faith and Gentlehood,
15 Of Service and Sacrifice;
    And it does not match our mood,
To turn so soon to your treacheries
    That starve our land of her food.

Our ears still carry the sound
20   Of our once-Imperial seas,
Exultant after our King was crowned,
    Beneath the sun and the breeze.
It is too early to have them bound
    Or sold at your decrees.

25   Wait till the memory goes,
          Wait till the visions fade.
      We may betray in time, God knows,
          But we would not have it said,
      When you make report to our scornful foes,
30   That we kissed as we betrayed!

The Female of the Species

When the Himalayan peasant meets the he-bear in his
                pride,
He shouts to scare the monster, who will often turn aside.
But the she-bear thus accosted rends the peasant tooth and
                nail.
For the female of the species is more deadly than the male.

5   When Nag the basking cobra hears the careless foot of
                man,
He will sometimes wriggle sideways and avoid it if he can.
But his mate makes no such motion where she camps
                beside the trail.
For the female of the species is more deadly than the male.

When the early Jesuit fathers preached to Hurons and
                Choctaws,
10   They prayed to be delivered from the vengeance of the
                squaws.
'Twas the women, not the warriors, turned those stark
                enthusiasts pale.
For the female of the species is more deadly than the male.

Man's timid heart is bursting with the things he must not
                say,
For the Woman that God gave him isn't his to give
                away;
15   But when the hunter meets with husband, each confirms
                the other's tale –
The female of the species is more deadly than the male.

Man, a bear in most relations – worm and savage
          otherwise, –
Man propounds negotiations, Man accepts the
          compromise.
Very rarely will he squarely push the logic of a fact
20   To its ultimate conclusion in unmitigated act.

Fear, or foolishness, impels him, ere he lay the wicked low,
To concede some form of trial even to his fiercest foe.
Mirth obscene diverts his anger – Doubt and Pity oft
          perplex
Him in dealing with an issue – to the scandal of The Sex!

25   But the Woman that God gave him, every fibre of her
          frame
Proves her launched for one sole issue, armed and engined
          for the same;
And to serve that single issue, lest the generations fail,
The female of the species must be deadlier than the male.

She who faces death by torture for each life beneath her
          breast
30   May not deal in doubt or pity – must not swerve for fact or
          jest.
These be purely male diversions – not in these her honour
          dwells.
She the Other Law we live by, is that Law and nothing
          else.

She can bring no more to living than the powers that make
          her great
As the Mother of the Infant and the Mistress of the Mate!
35   And when Babe and Man are lacking and she strides
          unclaimed to claim
Her right as femme (and baron), her equipment is the
          same.

She is wedded to convictions – in default of grosser ties;
Her contentions are her children, Heaven help him who
          denies! –

He will meet no suave discussion, but the instant, white-
        hot, wild,
40   Wakened female of the species warring as for spouse and
        child.

Unprovoked and awful charges – even so the she-bear fights,
Speech that drips, corrodes, and poisons – even so the
        cobra bites;
Scientific vivisection of one nerve till it is raw
And the victim writhes in anguish – like the Jesuit with the
        squaw!

45   So it comes that Man, the coward, when he gathers to confer
With his fellow-braves in council, dare not leave a place for her
Where, at war with Life and Conscience, he uplifts his
        erring hands
To some God of Abstract Justice – which no woman
        understands.

And Man knows it! Knows, moreover, that the woman that
        God gave him
50   Must command but may not govern – shall enthral but not
        enslave him.
And *She* knows, because She warns him, and Her instincts
        never fail,
That the Female of Her Species is more deadly than the Male!

The River's Tale

(PREHISTORIC)

Twenty bridges from Tower to Kew –
(Twenty bridges or twenty-two) –
Wanted to know what the River knew,
For they were young and the Thames was old,
5   *And this is the tale that the River told: –*

I walk my beat before London Town,
Five hours up and seven down.
Up I go till I end my run
At Tide-end-town, which is Teddington.
10 Down I come with the mud in my hands
And plaster it over the Maplin Sands.
But I'd have you know that these waters of mine
Were once a branch of the River Rhine,
When hundreds of miles to the East I went
15 And England was joined to the Continent.

I remember the bat-winged lizard-birds,
The Age of Ice and the Mammoth herds,
And the Giant Tigers that stalked them down
Through Regent's Park into Camden Town.
20 And I remember like yesterday
The earliest Cockney who came my way,
When he pushed through the forest that lined the Strand,
With paint on his face and a club in his hand.
He was death to feather and fin and fur.
25 He trapped my beavers at Westminster.
He netted my salmon, he hunted my deer,
He killed my heron off Lambeth Pier.
He fought his neighbour with axes and swords,
Flint or bronze, at my upper fords,
30 While down at Greenwich, for slaves and tin,
The tall Phoenician ships stole in,
And North Sea war-boats, painted and gay,
Flashed like dragon-flies, Erith way;
And Norseman, Negro and Gaul and Greek
35 Drank with the Britons in Barking Creek,
And life was gay, and the world was new,
And I was a mile across at Kew!
But the Roman came with a heavy hand,
And bridged and roaded and ruled the land,
40 And the Roman left and the Danes blew in —
And that's where your history-books begin!

The Roman Centurion's Song

(ROMAN OCCUPATION OF BRITAIN, A.D. 300)

Legate, I had the news last night – my cohort ordered home
By ship to Portus Itius and thence by road to Rome.
I've marched the companies aboard, the arms are stowed
    below:
Now let another take my sword. Command me not to go!

5   I've served in Britain forty years, from Vectis to the Wall.
I have none other home than this, nor any life at all.
Last night I did not understand, but, now the hour draws
    near
That calls me to my native land, I feel that land is here.

Here where men say my name was made, here where my
    work was done;
10 Here where my dearest dead are laid – my wife – my wife
    and son;
Here, where time, custom, grief and toil, age, memory,
    service, love,
Have rooted me in British soil. Ah, how can I remove?

For me this land, that sea, these airs, those folk and fields
    suffice.
What purple Southern pomp can match our changeful
    Northern skies,
15 Black with December snows unshed or pearled with August
    haze –
The changing arch of steel-grey March, or June's long-
    lighted days?

You'll follow widening Rhodanus till vine and olive lean
Aslant before the sunny breeze that sweeps Nemausus
    clean
To Arelate's triple gate; but let me linger on,
20 Here where our stiff-necked British oaks confront
    Euroclydon!

You'll take the old Aurelian Road through shore-descending
      pines
Where, blue as any peacock's neck, the Tyrrhene Ocean
      shines.
You'll go where laurel crowns are won, but – will you e'er
      forget
The scent of hawthorn in the sun, or bracken in the wet?

25   Let me work here for Britain's sake – at any task you will –
A marsh to drain, a road to make or native troops to drill.
Some Western camp (I know the Pict) or granite Border
      keep,
Mid seas of heather derelict, where our old messmates
      sleep.

Legate, I come to you in tears – My cohort ordered home!
30   I've served in Britain forty years. What should I do in Rome?
Here is my heart, my soul, my mind – the only life I know.
I cannot leave it all behind. Command me not to go!

Dane-Geld

It is always a temptation to an armed and agile nation
    To call upon a neighbour and to say: –
'We invaded you last night – we are quite prepared to
      fight,
    Unless you pay us cash to go away.'

5   And that is called asking for Dane-geld,
    And the people who ask it explain
That you've only to pay 'em the Dane-geld
    And then you'll get rid of the Dane!

It is always a temptation to a rich and lazy nation,
10   To puff and look important and to say: –
'Though we know we should defeat you, we have not the
      time to meet you.
We will therefore pay you cash to go away.'

And that is called paying the Dane-geld;
 But we've proved it again and again,
15 That if once you have paid him the Dane-geld
 You never get rid of the Dane.

It is wrong to put temptation in the path of any nation,
 For fear they should succumb and go astray;
So when you are requested to pay up or be molested,
20 You will find it better policy to say: –

'We never pay *any*-one Dane-geld,
 No matter how trifling the cost;
For the end of that game is oppression and shame,
 And the nation that plays it is lost!'

The French Wars

The boats of Newhaven and Folkestone and Dover
To Dieppe and Boulogne and to Calais cross over;
And in each of those runs there is not a square yard
Where the English and French haven't fought and fought
     hard!

5 If the ships that were sunk could be floated once more,
They'd stretch like a raft from the shore to the shore,
And we'd see, as we crossed, every pattern and plan
Of ship that was built since sea-fighting began.

There'd be biremes and brigantines, cutters and sloops,
10 Cogs, carracks and galleons with gay gilded poops –
Hoys, caravels, ketches, corvettes and the rest,
As thick as regattas, from Ramsgate to Brest.

But the galleys of Caesar, the squadrons of Sluys,
And Nelson's crack frigates are hid from our eyes,
15 Where the high Seventy-fours of Napoleon's days
Lie down with Deal luggers and French *chasse-marées*.

They'll answer no signal – they rest on the ooze,
With their honey-combed guns and their skeleton crews –
And racing above them, through sunshine or gale,
20 The Cross-Channel packets come in with the Mail.

Then the poor sea-sick passengers, English and French,
Must open their trunks on the Custom-house bench,
While the officers rummage for smuggled cigars
And nobody thinks of our blood-thirsty wars!

The Glory of the Garden

Our England is a garden that is full of stately views,
Of borders, beds and shrubberies and lawns and avenues,
With statues on the terraces and peacocks strutting by;
But the Glory of the Garden lies in more than meets the
      eye.

5 For where the old thick laurels grow, along the thin red
      wall,
You find the tool- and potting-sheds which are the heart of
      all;
The cold-frames and the hot-houses, the dungpits and the
      tanks,
The rollers, carts and drain-pipes, with the barrows and
      the planks.

And there you'll see the gardeners, the men and 'prentice
      boys
10 Told off to do as they are bid and do it without noise;
For, except when seeds are planted and we shout to scare
      the birds,
The Glory of the Garden it abideth not in words.

And some can pot begonias and some can bud a rose,
And some are hardly fit to trust with anything that grows;

15   But they can roll and trim the lawns and sift the sand and loam,
     For the Glory of the Garden occupieth all who come.

     Our England is a garden, and such gardens are not made
     By singing: – 'Oh, how beautiful!' and sitting in the shade,
     While better men than we go out and start their working
                                                    lives
20   At grubbing weeds from gravel-paths with broken dinner-
                                                    knives.

     There's not a pair of legs so thin, there's not a head so thick,
     There's not a hand so weak and white, nor yet a heart so
                                                    sick,
     But it can find some needful job that's crying to be done,
     For the Glory of the Garden glorifieth every one.

25   Then seek your job with thankfulness and work till further
                                                    orders,
     If it's only netting strawberries or killing slugs on borders;
     And when your back stops aching and your hands begin to
                                                    harden,
     You will find yourself a partner in the Glory of the Garden.

     Oh, Adam was a gardener, and God who made him sees
30   That half a proper gardener's work is done upon his knees,
     So when your work is finished, you can wash your hands
                                                    and pray
     For the Glory of the Garden, that it may not pass away!
     And the Glory of the Garden it shall never pass away!

     ## 'For All We Have and Are'

     ### 1914

     For all we have and are,
     For all our children's fate,
     Stand up and take the war.
     The Hun is at the gate!

5   Our world has passed away,
In wantonness o'erthrown.
There is nothing left to-day
But steel and fire and stone!
     Though all we knew depart,
10   The old Commandments stand: –
     'In courage keep your heart,
     In strength lift up your hand.'

Once more we hear the word
That sickened earth of old: –
15   'No law except the Sword
Unsheathed and uncontrolled.'
Once more it knits mankind,
Once more the nations go
To meet and break and bind
20   A crazed and driven foe.

Comfort, content, delight,
The ages' slow-bought gain,
They shrivelled in a night.
Only ourselves remain
25   To face the naked days
In silent fortitude,
Through perils and dismays
Renewed and re-renewed.
     Though all we made depart,
30   The old Commandments stand: –
     'In patience keep your heart,
     In strength lift up your hand.'

No easy hope or lies
Shall bring us to our goal,
35   But iron sacrifice
Of body, will, and soul.
There is but one task for all –
One life for each to give.
What stands if Freedom fall?
40   Who dies if England live?

Mine Sweepers

1914–18

Dawn off the Foreland – the young flood making
    Jumbled and short and steep –
Black in the hollows and bright where it's breaking –
    Awkward water to sweep.
5   'Mines reported in the fairway,
Warn all traffic and detain.
Sent up *Unity*, *Claribel*, *Assyrian*, *Stormcock*, and *Golden
        Gain*.'

Noon off the Foreland – the first ebb making
    Lumpy and strong in the bight.
10   Boom after boom, and the golf-hut shaking
    And the jackdaws wild with fright!
      'Mines located in the fairway,
    Boats now working up the chain.
Sweepers – *Unity*, *Claribel*, *Assyrian*, *Stormcock*, and *Golden
        Gain*.'

15   Dusk off the Foreland – the last light going
    And the traffic crowding through,
And five damned trawlers with their syreens blowing
    Heading the whole review!
      'Sweep completed in the fairway.
20   No more mines remain.
Sent back *Unity*, *Claribel*, *Assyrian*, *Stormcock*, and *Golden
        Gain*.'

'Tin Fish'

1914–18

The ships destroy us above
    And ensnare us beneath.
We arise, we lie down, and we move
    In the belly of Death.

5   The ships have a thousand eyes
       To mark where we come . . .
    But the mirth of a seaport dies
       When our blow gets home.

'The Trade'

(SUBMARINES)

They bear, in place of classic names,
    Letters and numbers on their skin.
They play their grisly blindfold games
    In little boxes made of tin.
5   Sometimes they stalk the Zeppelin,
Sometimes they learn where mines are laid,
    Or where the Baltic ice is thin.
That is the custom of 'The Trade.'

Few prize-courts sit upon their claims.
10   They seldom tow their targets in.
They follow certain secret aims
    Down under, far from strife or din.
    When they are ready to begin
No flag is flown, no fuss is made
15   More than the shearing of a pin.
That is the custom of 'The Trade.'

The Scout's quadruple funnel flames
    A mark from Sweden to the Swin,
The Cruiser's thund'rous screw proclaims
20   Her comings out and goings in:
    But only whiffs of paraffin
Or creamy rings that fizz and fade
    Show where the one-eyed Death has been.
That is the custom of 'The Trade.'

25   Their feats, their fortunes and their fames
      Are hidden from their nearest kin;
No eager public backs or blames,
      No journal prints the yarn they spin
      (The Censor would not let it in!)
30   When they return from run or raid.
      Unheard they work, unseen they win.
That is the custom of 'The Trade.'

'My Boy Jack'

1914–18

'Have you news of my boy Jack?'
    Not this tide.
'When d'you think that he'll come back?'
    Not with this wind blowing, and this tide.

5   'Has any one else had word of him?'
    Not this tide.
For what is sunk will hardly swim,
    Not with this wind blowing, and this tide.

'Oh, dear, what comfort can I find?'
10   *None this tide,*
    Nor any tide,
Except he did not shame his kind –
    Not even with that wind blowing, and that tide.

Then hold your head up all the more,
15   *This tide,*
    And every tide;
Because he was the son you bore,
    And gave to that wind blowing and that tide!

The Question

1916

Brethren, how shall it fare with me
    When the war is laid aside,
If it be proven that I am he
    For whom a world has died?

5   If it be proven that all my good,
    And the greater good I will make,
Were purchased me by a multitude
    Who suffered for my sake?

That I was delivered by mere mankind
10   Vowed to one sacrifice,
And not, as I hold them, battle-blind,
    But dying with open eyes?

That they did not ask me to draw the sword
    When they stood to endure their lot –
15 That they only looked to me for a word,
    And I answered I knew them not?

If it be found, when the battle clears,
    Their death has set me free,
Then how shall I live with myself through the years
20   Which they have bought for me?

Brethren, how must it fare with me,
    Or how am I justified,
If it be proven that I am he
    For whom mankind has died –
25 If it be proven that I am he
    Who, being questioned, denied?

Mesopotamia

1917

They shall not return to us, the resolute, the young,
    The eager and whole-hearted whom we gave:
But the men who left them thriftily to die in their own dung,
    Shall they come with years and honour to the grave?

5   They shall not return to us, the strong men coldly slain
        In sight of help denied from day to day:
But the men who edged their agonies and chid them in
            their pain,
    Are they too strong and wise to put away?

Our dead shall not return to us while Day and Night
            divide –
10   Never while the bars of sunset hold.
But the idle-minded overlings who quibbled while they
            died,
    Shall they thrust for high employments as of old?

Shall we only threaten and be angry for an hour?
    When the storm is ended shall we find
15   How softly but how swiftly they have sidled back to power
    By the favour and contrivance of their kind?

Even while they soothe us, while they promise large
            amends,
    Even while they make a show of fear,
Do they call upon their debtors, and take counsel with
            their friends,
20   To confirm and re-establish each career?

Their lives cannot repay us – their death could not undo –
    The shame that they have laid upon our race.
But the slothfulness that wasted and the arrogance that slew,
    Shall we leave it unabated in its place?

The Holy War

1917

'For here lay the excellent wisdom of him that built Mansoul, that the walls could never be broken down nor hurt by the most mighty adverse potentate unless the townsmen gave consent thereto.'

Bunyan's *Holy War*

A tinker out of Bedford,
    A vagrant oft in quod,
A private under Fairfax,
    A minister of God –
5 Two hundred years and thirty
    Ere Armageddon came
His single hand portrayed it,
    And Bunyan was his name!

He mapped for those who follow,
10   The world in which we are –
'This famous town of Mansoul'
    That takes the Holy War.
Her true and traitor people,
    The Gates along her wall,
15 From Eye Gate unto Feel Gate,
    John Bunyan showed them all.

All enemy divisions,
    Recruits of every class,
And highly screened positions
20   For flame or poison-gas;
The craft that we call modern,
    The crimes that we call new,
John Bunyan had 'em typed and filed
    In Sixteen Eighty-two.

25 Likewise the Lords of Looseness
    That hamper faith and works,
The Perseverance-Doubters,
    And Present-Comfort shirks,

With brittle intellectuals
30   Who crack beneath a strain –
John Bunyan met that helpful set
        In Charles the Second's reign.

Emmanuel's vanguard dying
        For right and not for rights,
35 My Lord Apollyon lying
        To the State-kept Stockholmites,
The Pope, the swithering Neutrals,
        The Kaiser and his Gott –
Their rôles, their goals, their naked souls –
40   He knew and drew the lot.

Now he hath left his quarters,
        In Bunhill Fields to lie,
The wisdom that he taught us
        Is proven prophecy –
45 One watchword through our Armies,
        One answer from our Lands: –
'No dealings with Diabolus
        As long as Mansoul stands!'

A pedlar from a hovel,
50   *The lowest of the low –*
The Father of the Novel,
        Salvation's first Defoe –
Eight blinded generations
        Ere Armageddon came,
55 *He showed us how to meet it,*
        And Bunyan was his name!

Jobson's Amen

'Blessèd be the English and all their ways and works.
Cursèd be the Infidels, Hereticks, and Turks!'
'Amen,' quo' Jobson, 'but where I used to lie
Was neither Candle, Bell nor Book to curse my brethren by:

5   'But a palm-tree in full bearing, bowing down, bowing
          down,
  To a surf that drove unsparing at the brown, walled town –
  Conches in a temple, oil-lamps in a dome –
  And a low moon out of Africa said: "This way home!"'

  'Blessèd be the English and all that they profess.
10   Cursèd be the Savages that prance in nakedness!'
  'Amen,' quo' Jobson, 'but where I used to lie
  Was neither shirt nor pantaloons to catch my brethren by:

  'But a well-wheel slowly creaking, going round, going
          round,
  By a water-channel leaking over drowned, warm ground –
15   Parrots very busy in the trellised pepper-vine –
  And a high sun over Asia shouting: "Rise and shine!"'

  'Blessèd be the English and everything they own.
  Cursèd be the Infidels that bow to wood and stone!'
  'Amen,' quo' Jobson, 'but where I used to lie
20   Was neither pew nor Gospelleer to save my brethren by:

  'But a desert stretched and stricken, left and right, left and
          right,
  Where the piled mirages thicken under white-hot light –
  A skull beneath a sand-hill and a viper coiled inside –
  And a red wind out of Libya roaring: "Run and hide!"'

25   'Blessèd be the English and all they make or do.
  Cursèd be the Hereticks who doubt that this is true!'
  'Amen,' quo' Jobson, 'but where I mean to die
  Is neither rule nor calliper to judge the matter by:

  'But Himàlaya heavenward-heading, sheer and vast, sheer
          and vast,
30   In a million summits bedding on the last world's past –
  A certain sacred mountain where the scented cedars climb,
  And – the feet of my Belovèd hurrying back through
          Time!'

The Fabulists

When all the world would keep a matter hid,
    Since Truth is seldom friend to any crowd,
Men write in fable, as old Aesop did,
    Jesting at that which none will name aloud.
5   And this they needs must do, or it will fall
Unless they please they are not heard at all.

When desperate Folly daily laboureth
    To work confusion upon all we have,
When diligent Sloth demandeth Freedom's death,
10   And banded Fear commandeth Honour's grave –
Even in that certain hour before the fall,
Unless men please they are not heard at all.

Needs must all please, yet some not all for need,
    Needs must all toil, yet some not all for gain;
15 But that men, taking pleasure, may take heed,
    Whom present toil shall snatch from later pain.
Thus some have toiled, but their reward was small
Since, though they pleased, they were not heard at all.

This was the lock that lay upon our lips,
20   This was the yoke that we have undergone.
Denying us all pleasant fellowships
    As in our time and generation.
Our pleasures unpursued age past recall,
And for our pains – we are not heard at all.

25 What man hears aught except the groaning guns?
    What man heeds aught save what each instant brings?
When each man's life all imaged life outruns,
    What man shall pleasure in imaginings?
So it hath fallen, as it was bound to fall,
30 We are not, nor we were not, heard at all!

Justice

OCTOBER 1918

Across a world where all men grieve
     And grieving strive the more,
The great days range like tides and leave
     Our dead on every shore.
5   *Heavy the load we undergo,*
     And our own hands prepare,
If we have parley with the foe,
     The load our sons must bear.

Before we loose the word
10   That bids new worlds to birth,
Needs must we loosen first the sword
     Of Justice upon earth;
Or else all else is vain
     Since life on earth began,
15 And the spent world sinks back again
     Hopeless of God and Man.

A people and their King
     Through ancient sin grown strong,
Because they feared no reckoning
20   Would set no bound to wrong;
But now their hour is past,
     And we who bore it find
Evil Incarnate held at last
     To answer to mankind.

25 For agony and spoil
     Of nations beat to dust,
For poisoned air and tortured soil
     And cold, commanded lust,
And every secret woe
30   The shuddering waters saw –
Willed and fulfilled by high and low –
     Let them relearn the Law:

That when the dooms are read,
   Not high nor low shall say: –
35 'My haughty or my humble head
   Has saved me in this day.'
That, till the end of time,
   Their remnant shall recall
Their fathers' old, confederate crime
40   Availed them not at all:

That neither schools nor priests,
   Nor Kings may build again
A people with the hearts of beasts
   Made wise concerning men.
45 Whereby our dead shall sleep
   In honour, unbetrayed,
And we in faith and honour keep
   That peace for which they paid.

The Hyaenas

After the burial-parties leave
   And the baffled kites have fled;
The wise hyaenas come out at eve
   To take account of our dead.

5 How he died and why he died
   Troubles them not a whit.
They snout the bushes and stones aside
   And dig till they come to it.

They are only resolute they shall eat
10   That they and their mates may thrive;
And they know that the dead are safer meat
   Than the weakest thing alive.

(For a goat may butt, and a worm may sting,
    And a child will sometimes stand;
15 But a poor dead soldier of the King
    Can never lift a hand.)

They whoop and halloo and scatter the dirt
    Until their tushes white
Take good hold of the Army shirt,
20   And tug the corpse to light,

And the pitiful face is shown again
    For an instant ere they close;
But it is not discovered to living men –
    Only to God and to those

25 Who, being soulless, are free from shame,
    Whatever meat they may find.
Nor do they defile the dead man's name –
    That is reserved for his kind.

En-Dor

(1914–19–?)

'Behold there is a woman that hath a familiar spirit at En-dor'
        I Samuel 28: 7

The road to En-dor is easy to tread
    For Mother or yearning Wife.
There, it is sure, we shall meet our Dead
    As they were even in life.
5 Earth has not dreamed of the blessing in store
For desolate hearts on the road to En-dor.

Whispers shall comfort us out of the dark –
    Hands – ah, God! – that we knew!
Visions and voices – look and hark! –
10   Shall prove that the tale is true,
And that those who have passed to the further shore
May be hailed – at a price – on the road to En-dor.

But they are so deep in their new eclipse
    Nothing they say can reach,
15 Unless it be uttered by alien lips
    And framed in a stranger's speech.
The son must send word to the mother that bore
Through an hireling's mouth. 'Tis the rule of
        En-dor.

And not for nothing these gifts are shown
20   By such as delight our Dead.
They must twitch and stiffen and slaver and groan
    Ere the eyes are set in the head,
And the voice from the belly begins. Therefore,
We pay them a wage where they ply at En-dor.

25 Even so, we have need of faith
    And patience to follow the clue.
Often, at first, what the dear one saith
    Is babble, or jest, or untrue.
(Lying spirits perplex us sore
30 Till our loves – and their lives – are well known at En-
        dor) . . .

Oh, the road to En-dor is the oldest road
    And the craziest road of all!
Straight it runs to the Witch's abode,
    As it did in the days of Saul.
35 *And nothing has changed of the sorrow in store*
For such as go down on the road to En-dor!

Gethsemane

1914–18

The Garden called Gethsemane
    In Picardy it was,
And there the people came to see
    The English soldiers pass.
5 We used to pass – we used to pass
    Or halt, as it might be,
And ship our masks in case of gas
    Beyond Gethsemane.

The Garden called Gethsemane,
10   It held a pretty lass,
But all the time she talked to me
    I prayed my cup might pass.
The officer sat on the chair,
    The men lay on the grass,
15 And all the time we halted there
    I prayed my cup might pass.

It didn't pass – it didn't pass –
    It didn't pass from me.
I drank it when we met the gas
20   Beyond Gethsemane!

The Craftsman

Once, after long-drawn revel at The Mermaid,
He to the overbearing Boanerges,
Jonson, uttered (if half of it were liquor,
       Blessed be the vintage!)

5   Saying how, at an alehouse under Cotswold,
He had made sure of his very Cleopatra
Drunk with enormous, salvation-contemning
           Love for a tinker.

How, while he hid from Sir Thomas's keepers,
10   Crouched in a ditch and drenched by the midnight
Dews, he had listened to gipsy Juliet
           Rail at the dawning.

How at Bankside, a boy drowning kittens
Winced at the business; whereupon his sister –
15   Lady Macbeth aged seven – thrust 'em under,
           Sombrely scornful.

How on a Sabbath, hushed and compassionate –
She being known since her birth to the townsfolk –
Stratford dredged and delivered from Avon
20   Dripping Ophelia.

So, with a thin third finger marrying
Drop to wine-drop domed on the table,
Shakespeare opened his heart till the sunrise
           Entered to hear him.

25   London waked and he, imperturbable,
Passed from waking to hurry after shadows . . .
Busied upon shows of no earthly importance?
           Yes, but he knew it!

The Benefactors

Ah! What avails the classic bent
   And what the cultured word,
Against the undoctored incident
   That actually occurred?

5   *And what is Art whereto we press*
          Through paint and prose and rhyme –
      When Nature in her nakedness
          Defeats us every time?

      It is not learning, grace nor gear,
10   Nor easy meat and drink,
      But bitter pinch of pain and fear
          That makes creation think.

      When in this world's unpleasing youth
          Our god-like race began,
15   The longest arm, the sharpest tooth,
          Gave man control of man;

      Till, bruised and bitten to the bone
          And taught by pain and fear,
      He learned to deal the far-off stone,
20   And poke the long, safe spear.

      So tooth and nail were obsolete
          As means against a foe,
      Till, bored by uniform defeat,
          Some genius built the bow.

25   Then stone and javelin proved as vain
          As old-time tooth and nail,
      Till, spurred anew by fear and pain,
          Man fashioned coats of mail.

      Then was there safety for the rich
30   And danger for the poor,
      Till someone mixed a powder which
          Redressed the scale once more.

      Helmet and armour disappeared
          With sword and bow and pike,
35   And, when the smoke of battle cleared,
          All men were armed alike . . .

And when ten million such were slain
    To please one crazy king,
Man, schooled in bulk by fear and pain,
40   Grew weary of the thing;

And, at the very hour designed,
    To enslave him past recall,
His tooth-stone-arrow-gun-shy mind
    Turned and abolished all.

45 *All Power, each Tyrant, every Mob*
    Whose head has grown too large,
Ends by destroying its own job
    And earns its own discharge;

And Man, whose mere necessities
50   *Move all things from his path,*
Trembles meanwhile at their decrees,
    And deprecates their wrath!

Natural Theology

PRIMITIVE

I ate my fill of a whale that died
    And stranded after a month at sea . . .
There is a pain in my inside.
    Why have the Gods afflicted me?
5 Ow! I am purged till I am a wraith!
    Wow! I am sick till I cannot see!
What is the sense of Religion and Faith?
    Look how the Gods have afflicted me!

PAGAN

How can the skin of rat or mouse hold
10   Anything more than a harmless flea? . . .
The burning plague has taken my household.
    Why have my Gods afflicted me?

All my kith and kin are deceased,
   Though they were as good as good could be.
15 I will out and batter the family priest,
   Because my Gods have afflicted me!

MEDIAEVAL

My privy and well drain into each other
   After the custom of Christendie . . .
Fevers and fluxes are wasting my mother.
20   Why has the Lord afflicted me?
The Saints are helpless for all I offer –
   So are the clergy I used to fee.
Henceforward I keep my cash in my coffer,
   Because the Lord has afflicted me.

MATERIAL

25 I run eight hundred hens to the acre.
   They die by dozens mysteriously . . .
I am more than doubtful concerning my Maker.
   Why has the Lord afflicted me?
What a return for all my endeavour –
30   Not to mention the L.S.D.!
I am an atheist now and for ever,
   Because this God has afflicted me!

PROGRESSIVE

Money spent on an Army or Fleet
   Is homicidal lunacy . . .
35 My son has been killed in the Mons retreat.
   Why is the Lord afflicting me?
Why are murder, pillage and arson
   And rape allowed by the Deity?
I will write to the *Times*, deriding our parson,
40   Because my God has afflicted me.

CHORUS

We had a kettle: we let it leak:
  Our not repairing it made it worse.
We haven't had any tea for a week . . .
  The bottom is out of the Universe!

CONCLUSION

45 This was none of the good Lord's pleasure,
      For the Spirit He breathed in Man is free;
    But what comes after is measure for measure
      And not a God that afflicteth thee.
    As was the sowing so the reaping
50   Is now and evermore shall be.
    Thou art delivered to thine own keeping.
      Only Thyself hath afflicted thee!

Epitaphs of the War

1914–18

'EQUALITY OF SACRIFICE'

A. 'I was a "have". B. 'I was a "have-not".'
  (*Together*.) 'What hast thou given which I gave not?'

A SERVANT

We were together since the War began.
He was my servant – and the better man.

A SON

My son was killed while laughing at some jest. I would I
                  knew
What it was, and it might serve me in a time when jests are
                  few.

AN ONLY SON

I have slain none except my Mother. She
(Blessing her slayer) died of grief for me.

EX-CLERK

Pity not! The Army gave
Freedom to a timid slave:
In which Freedom did he find
Strength of body, will, and mind:
By which strength he came to prove
Mirth, Companionship, and Love:
For which Love to Death he went:
In which Death he lies content.

THE WONDER

Body and Spirit I surrendered whole
To harsh Instructors – and received a soul . . .
If mortal man could change me through and through
From all I was – what may The God not do?

HINDU SEPOY IN FRANCE

This man in his own country prayed we know not to what
                    Powers.
We pray Them to reward him for his bravery in ours.

THE COWARD

I could not look on Death, which being known,
Men led me to him, blindfold and alone.

SHOCK

My name, my speech, my self I had forgot.
My wife and children came – I knew them not.
I died. My Mother followed. At her call
And on her bosom I remembered all.

A GRAVE NEAR CAIRO

Gods of the Nile, should this stout fellow here
Get out – get out! He knows not shame nor fear.

PELICANS IN THE WILDERNESS
A Grave near Halfa

The blown sand heaps on me, that none may learn
    Where I am laid for whom my children grieve . . .
O wings that beat at dawning, ye return
    Out of the desert to your young at eve!

'CANADIANS'

We, giving all, gained all.
    Neither lament us nor praise;
Only, in all things recall,
    It is fear, not death, that slays.

INSCRIPTION ON MEMORIAL IN SAULT
STE. MARIE, ONTARIO

From little towns in a far land, we came,
To save our honour, and a world aflame;
By little towns in a far land, we sleep
And trust those things we won, to you to keep.

THE FAVOUR

Death favoured me from the first, well knowing I could
                not endure
    To wait on him day by day. He quitted my betters
                and came
Whistling over the fields, and, when he had made all sure,
    'Thy line is at end,' he said, 'but at least I have saved
                its name.'

THE BEGINNER

On the first hour of my first day
    In the front trench I fell.
(Children in boxes at a play
    Stand up to watch it well.)

R.A.F. (AGE EIGHTEEN)

Laughing through clouds, his milk-teeth still unshed,
Cities and men he smote from overhead.
His deaths delivered, he returned to play
Childlike, with childish things now put away.

THE REFINED MAN

I was of delicate mind. I went aside for my needs,
    Disdaining the common office. I was seen from afar and
        killed . . .
How is this matter for mirth? Let each man be judged by
        his deeds.
    *I have paid my price to live with myself on the terms that
        I willed.*

NATIVE WATER-CARRIER (M.E.F.)

Prometheus brought down fire to men.
    This brought up water.
The Gods are jealous – now, as then,
    Giving no quarter.

BOMBED IN LONDON

On land and sea I strove with anxious care
To escape conscription. It was in the air!

THE SLEEPY SENTINEL

Faithless the watch that I kept: now I have none to keep.
I was slain because I slept: now I am slain I sleep.
Let no man reproach me again, whatever watch is unkept –
I sleep because I am slain. They slew me because I slept.

BATTERIES OUT OF AMMUNITION

If any mourn us in the workshop, say,
We died because the shift kept holiday.

COMMON FORM

If any question why we died.
Tell them, because our fathers lied.

A DEAD STATESMAN

I could not dig: I dared not rob:
Therefore I lied to please the mob.
Now all my lies are proved untrue
And I must face the men I slew.
What tale shall serve me here among
Mine angry and defrauded young?

THE REBEL

If I had clamoured at Thy Gate
    For the gift of Life on Earth,
And, thrusting through the souls that wait
    Flung headlong into birth –
Even then, even then, for gin and snare
    About my pathway spread,
Lord, I had mocked Thy thoughtful care
    Before I joined the Dead!
But now? . . . I was beneath Thy Hand
    Ere yet the Planets came.
And now – though Planets pass, I stand
    The witness to Thy shame!

THE OBEDIENT

Daily, though no ears attended,
    Did my prayers arise.
Daily, though no fire descended,
    Did I sacrifice.

Though my darkness did not lift,
   Though I faced no lighter odds,
Though the Gods bestowed no gift,
      None the less,
   None the less, I served the Gods!

A DRIFTER OFF TARENTUM

He from the wind-bitten North with ship and companions
        descended,
   Searching for eggs of death spawned by invisible hulls.
Many he found and drew forth. Of a sudden the fishery
        ended
   In flame and a clamorous breath known to the eye-
        pecking gulls.

DESTROYERS IN COLLISION

For Fog and Fate no charm is found
   To lighten or amend.
I, hurrying to my bride, was drowned –
   Cut down by my best friend.

CONVOY ESCORT

I was a shepherd to fools
   Causelessly bold or afraid.
They would not abide by my rules.
   Yet they escaped. For I stayed.

UNKNOWN FEMALE CORPSE

Headless, lacking foot and hand,
Horrible I come to land.
I beseech all women's sons
Know I was a mother once.

RAPED AND REVENGED

One used and butchered me: another spied
Me broken – for which thing an hundred died.
So it was learned among the heathen hosts
How much a freeborn woman's favour costs.

SALONIKAN GRAVE

I have watched a thousand days
Push out and crawl into night
Slowly as tortoises.
Now I, too, follow these.
It is fever, and not the fight –
Time, not battle, – that slays.

THE BRIDEGROOM

Call me not false, beloved,
    If, from thy scarce-known breast
So little time removed,
    In other arms I rest.

For this more ancient bride,
    Whom coldly I embrace,
Was constant at my side
    Before I saw thy face.

Our marriage, often set –
    By miracle delayed –
At last is consummate
    And cannot be unmade.

Live, then, whom Life shall cure,
    Almost, of Memory,
And leave us to endure
    Its immortality.

V.A.D (MEDITERRANEAN)

Ah, would swift ships had never been, for then we ne'er
          had found,
These harsh Aegean rocks between, this little virgin
          drowned,
Whom neither spouse nor child shall mourn, but men she
          nursed through pain
And – certain keels for whose return the heathen look in vain.

ACTORS
On a Memorial Tablet in Holy Trinity Church,
Stratford-on-Avon

We counterfeited once for your disport
   Men's joy and sorrow: but our day has passed.
We pray you pardon all where we fell short –
   Seeing we were your servants to this last.

JOURNALISTS
On a Panel in the Hall of the Institute of Journalists

We have served our day.

The Gods of the Copybook Headings

As I pass through my incarnations in every age and race,
I make my proper prostrations to the Gods of the Market-
          Place.
Peering through reverent fingers I watch them flourish and
          fall,
And the Gods of the Copybook Headings, I notice, outlast
          them all.

5   We were living in trees when they met us. They showed us
          each in turn
That Water would certainly wet us, as Fire would certainly
          burn:

But we found them lacking in Uplift, Vision and Breadth
of Mind,
So we left them to teach the Gorillas while we followed the
March of Mankind.

We moved as the Spirit listed. *They* never altered their pace,
10 Being neither cloud nor wind-borne like the Gods of the
Market-Place,
But they always caught up with our progress, and presently
word would come
That a tribe had been wiped off its icefield, or the lights
had gone out in Rome.

With the Hopes that our World is built on they were
utterly out of touch,
They denied that the Moon was Stilton; they denied she
was even Dutch;
15 They denied that Wishes were Horses; they denied that a
Pig had Wings;
So we worshipped the Gods of the Market Who promised
these beautiful things.

When the Cambrian measures were forming, They
promised perpetual peace.
They swore, if we gave them our weapons, that the wars of
the tribes would cease.
But when we disarmed They sold us and delivered us
bound to our foe,
20 And the Gods of the Copybook Headings said: '*Stick to the
Devil you know.*'

On the first Feminian Sandstones we were promised the
Fuller Life
(Which started by loving our neighbour and ended by
loving his wife)
Till our women had no more children and the men lost
reason and faith,
And the Gods of the Copybook Headings said: '*The Wages
of Sin is Death.*'

25   In the Carboniferous Epoch we were promised abundance
                for all,
      By robbing selected Peter to pay for collective Paul;
      But, though we had plenty of money, there was nothing
                our money could buy,
      And the Gods of the Copybook Headings said: '*If you don't
                work you die.*'

      Then the Gods of the Market tumbled, and their smooth-
                tongued wizards withdrew,
30   And the hearts of the meanest were humbled and began to
                believe it was true
      That All is not Gold that Glitters, and Two and Two make
                Four –
      And the Gods of the Copybook Headings limped up to
                explain it once more.

                 .   .   .   .   .   .

      As it will be in the future, it was at the birth of Man –
      There are only four things certain since Social Progress
                began: –
35   That the Dog returns to his Vomit and the Sow returns to
                her Mire,
      And the burnt Fool's bandaged finger goes wabbling back
                to the Fire;

      And that after this is accomplished, and the brave new
                world begins
      When all men are paid for existing and no man must pay
                for his sins,
      As surely as Water will wet us, as surely as Fire will burn,
40   The Gods of the Copybook Headings with terror and
                slaughter return!

The Clerks and the Bells

(OXFORD IN 1920)

The Merry clerks of Oxenford they stretch themselves at
     ease
Unhelmeted on unbleached sward beneath unshrivelled trees,
For the leaves, the leaves, are on the bough, the bark is on
     the bole,
And East and West men's housen stand all even-roofed and
     whole . . .
5   (*Men's housen doored and glazed and floored and whole at
     every turn!*)
And so the Bells of Oxenford ring: – 'Time it is to learn!'

The merry clerks of Oxenford they read and they are told
Of famous men who drew the sword in furious fights of
     old.
They heark and mark it faithfully, but never clerk will
     write
10   What vision rides 'twixt book and eye from any nearer
     fight.
     (*Whose supplication rends the soul? Whose night-long cries
     repeat?*)
And so the Bells of Oxenford ring: – 'Time it is to eat!'

The merry clerks of Oxenford they sit them down anon
At tables fair with silver-ware and naperies thereon,
15   Free to refuse or dainty choose what dish shall seem them
     good;
For they have done with single meats, and waters streaked
     with blood . . .
     (*That three days' fast is overpast when all those guns said
     'Nay'!*)
And so the Bells of Oxenford ring: – 'Time it is to play!'

The merry clerks of Oxenford they hasten one by one
20   Or band in companies abroad to ride, or row, or run

By waters level with fair meads all goldenly bespread,
Where flash June's clashing dragon-flies – but no man
        bows his head,
(*Though bullet-wise June's dragon-flies deride the fearless
        air!*)
And so the Bells of Oxenford ring: 'Time it is for prayer!'

25   The pious clerks of Oxenford they kneel at twilight-tide
For to receive and well believe the Word of Him Who
        died.
And, though no present wings of Death hawk hungry
        round that place,
Their brows are bent upon their hands that none may see
        their face –
(*Who set aside the world and died? What life shall please Him
        best?*)
30   And so the Bells of Oxenford ring: 'Time it is to rest!'

The merry clerks of Oxenford lie under bolt and bar
Lest they should rake the midnight clouds or chase a
        sliding star.
In fear of fine and dread rebuke, they round their full-
        night sleep,
And leave that world which once they took for older men
        to keep,
35   (*Who walks by dreams what ghostly wood in search of
        playmate slain?*)
Until the Bells of Oxenford ring in the light again.

Unburdened breeze, unstricken trees, and all God's works
        restored –
In this way live the merry clerks – the clerks of Oxenford!

Lollius

HORACE, BK V, ODE 13

Why gird at Lollius if he care
 To purchase in the city's sight,
With nard and roses for his hair,
 The name of Knight?

5 Son of unmitigated sires
 Enriched by trade in Afric corn,
His wealth allows, his wife requires,
 Him to be born.

Him slaves shall serve with zeal renewed
10 At lesser wage for longer whiles,
And school- and station-masters rude
 Receive with smiles.

His bowels shall be sought in charge
 By learned doctors; all his sons
15 And nubile daughters shall enlarge
 Their horizons.

For fierce she-Britons, apt to smite
 Their upward-climbing sisters down,
Shall smooth their plumes and oft invite
20 The brood to town.

For these delights will he disgorge
 The State enormous benefice,
But – by the head of either George –
 He pays not twice!

25 Whom neither lust for public pelf,
 Nor itch to make orations, vex –
Content to honour his own self
 With his own cheques –

That man is clean. At least, his house
30   Springs cleanly from untainted gold –
Not from a conscience or a spouse
      Sold and resold.

Time was, you say, before men knew
      Such arts, and rose by Virtue guided? . . .
35 The tables rock with laughter – you
      Not least derided.

London Stone

11 NOVEMBER, 1923

When you come to London Town,
      (Grieving – grieving!)
Bring your flowers and lay them down
      At the place of grieving.

5   When you come to London Town,
      (Grieving – grieving!)
Bow your head and mourn your own,
      With the others grieving.

For those minutes, let it wake
10   (Grieving – grieving!)
All the empty-heart and ache
      That is not cured by grieving.

For those minutes, tell no lie:
      (Grieving – grieving!)
15 'Grave, this is thy victory:
      And the sting of death is grieving.'

Where's our help, from Earth or Heaven.
      (Grieving – grieving!)
To comfort us for what we've given,
20   And only gained the grieving?

Heaven's too far and Earth too near,
    (Grieving – grieving!)
But our neighbour's standing here,
    Grieving as we're grieving.

25 What's his burden every day?
    (Grieving – grieving!)
Nothing man can count or weigh,
    But loss and love's own grieving.

What is the tie betwixt us two
30   (Grieving – grieving!)
That must last our whole lives through?
    '*As I suffer, so do you.*'
That may ease the grieving.

Doctors

Man dies too soon, beside his works half-planned.
    His days are counted and reprieve is vain:
Who shall entreat with Death to stay his hand;
    Or cloak the shameful nakedness of pain?

5 Send here the bold, the seekers of the way –
    The passionless, the unshakeable of soul,
Who serve the inmost mysteries of man's clay,
    And ask no more than leave to make them whole.

Chartres Windows

Colour fulfils where Music has no power:
    By each man's light the unjudging glass betrays
All men's surrender, each man's holiest hour
    And all the lit confusion of our days –
5 Purfled with iron, traced in dusk and fire,

Challenging ordered Time, who, at the last,
Shall bring it, grozed and leaded and wedged fast,
To the cold stone that curbs or crowns desire.
Yet on the pavement that all feet have trod –
10   Even as the Spirit, in her deeps and heights,
Turns only, and that voiceless, to her God –
There falls no tincture from those anguished lights.
And Heaven's one light, behind them, striking through
Blazons what each man dreamed no other knew.

The Changelings

(R.N.V.R.)

Or ever the battered liners sank
      With their passengers to the dark,
I was head of a Walworth Bank,
      And you were a grocer's clerk.

5   I was a dealer in stocks and shares,
      And you in butters and teas;
And we both abandoned our own affairs
      And took to the dreadful seas.

Wet and worry about our ways –
10   Panic, onset, and flight –
Had us in charge for a thousand days
      And a thousand-year-long night.

We saw more than the nights could hide –
      More than the waves could keep –
15   And – certain faces over the side
      Which do not go from our sleep.

We were more tired than words can tell
      While the pied craft fled by,
And the swinging mounds of the Western swell
20   Hoisted us heavens-high . . .

Now there is nothing – not even our rank –
    To witness what we have been;
And I am returned to my Walworth Bank,
    And you to your margarine!

Gipsy Vans

Unless you come of the gipsy stock
    That steals by night and day,
Lock your heart with a double lock
    And throw the key away.
5   Bury it under the blackest stone
        Beneath your father's hearth,
And keep your eyes on your lawful own
        And your feet to the proper path.
        Then you can stand at your door and mock
10   *When the gipsy vans come through . . .*
        For it isn't right that the Gorgio stock
        Should live as the Romany do.

Unless you come of the gipsy blood
    That takes and never spares,
15 Bide content with your given good
        And follow your own affairs.
Plough and harrow and roll your land,
        And sow what ought to be sowed;
But never let loose your heart from your hand,
20   Nor flitter it down the road!
        Then you can thrive on your boughten food
            As the gipsy vans come through . . .
        For it isn't nature the Gorgio blood
        Should love as the Romany do.

25 Unless you carry the gipsy eyes
        That see but seldom weep,
Keep your head from the naked skies
    Or the stars'll trouble your sleep.

Watch your moon through your window-pane
30   And take what weather she brews;
But don't run out in the midnight rain
       Nor home in the morning dews.
            Then you can huddle and shut your eyes
               As the gipsy vans come through . . .
35   *For it isn't fitting the Gorgio ryes*
               Should walk as the Romany do.

Unless you come of the gipsy race
       That counts all time the same,
Be you careful of Time and Place
40   And Judgment and Good Name:
Lose your life for to live your life
       The way that you ought to do;
And when you are finished, your God and your wife
       And the Gipsies'll laugh at you!
45   *Then you can rot in your burying-place*
               As the gipsy vans come through . . .
            For it isn't reason the Gorgio race
               Should die as the Romany do.

A Legend of Truth

Once on a time, the ancient legends tell,
Truth, rising from the bottom of her well,
Looked on the world, but, hearing how it lied,
Returned to her seclusion horrified.
5   There she abode, so conscious of her worth,
Not even Pilate's Question called her forth,
Nor Galileo, kneeling to deny
The Laws that hold our Planet 'neath the sky.
Meantime, her kindlier sister, whom men call
10 Fiction, did all her work and more than all,
With so much zeal, devotion, tact, and care,
That no one noticed Truth was otherwhere.

Then came a War when, bombed and gassed and mined,
Truth rose once more, perforce, to meet mankind,
15 And through the dust and glare and wreck of things,
Beheld a phantom on unbalanced wings,
Reeling and groping, dazed, dishevelled, dumb,
But semaphoring direr deeds to come.
Truth hailed and bade her stand; the quavering shade
20 Clung to her knees and babbled, 'Sister, aid!
I am – I was – thy Deputy, and men
Besought me for my useful tongue or pen
To gloss their gentle deeds, and I complied,
And they, and thy demands, were satisfied.
25 But this –' she pointed o'er the blistered plain,
Where men as Gods and Devils wrought amain –
'This is beyond me! Take thy work again.'

Tablets and pen transferred, she fled afar,
And Truth assumed the record of the War . . .
30 She saw, she heard, she read, she tried to tell
Facts beyond precedent and parallel –
Unfit to hint or breathe, much less to write,
But happening every minute, day and night.
She called for proof. It came. The dossiers grew.
35 She marked them, first, 'Return. This *can't* be true.'
Then, underneath the cold official word:
'This is not really half of what occurred.'

She faced herself at last, the story runs,
And telegraphed her sister: 'Come at once.
40 Facts out of hand. Unable overtake
Without your aid. Come back for Truth's own sake!
Co-equal rank and powers if you agree.
They need us both, but you far more than me!'

We and They

Father, Mother, and Me,
    Sister and Auntie say
All the people like us are We,
    And every one else is They.
5 And They live over the sea,
    While We live over the way,
But would you believe it? – They look upon We
    As only a sort of They!

We eat pork and beef
10   With cow-horn-handled knives.
They who gobble Their rice off a leaf
    Are horrified out of Their lives;
While They who live up a tree,
    And feast on grubs and clay,
15 (Isn't it scandalous?) look upon We
    As a simply disgusting They!

We shoot birds with a gun.
    They stick lions with spears.
Their full-dress is un-.
20   We dress up to Our ears.
They like Their friends for tea.
    We like Our friends to stay;
And, after all that, They look upon We
    As an utterly ignorant They!

25 We eat kitcheny food.
    We have doors that latch.
They drink milk or blood,
    Under an open thatch.
We have Doctors to fee.
30   They have Wizards to pay.
And (impudent heathen!) They look upon We
    As a quite impossible They!

All good people agree,
    And all good people say,
35   All nice people, like Us, are We,
    And every one else is They:
But if you cross over the sea,
    Instead of over the way,
You may end by (think of it!) looking on We
40   As only a sort of They!

Untimely

Nothing in life has been made by man for man's using
But it was shown long since to man in ages
Lost as the name of the maker of it,

Who received oppression and shame for his wages –
5 Hate, avoidance, and scorn in his daily dealings –
Until he perished, wholly confounded.

More to be pitied than he are the wise
Souls which foresaw the evil of loosing
Knowledge or Art before time, and aborted
10 Noble devices and deep-wrought healings,
Lest offence should arise.

Heaven delivers to Earth the Hour that cannot be
                thwarted,
Neither advanced, at the price of a world nor a soul, and
                its Prophet
Comes through the blood of the vanguards who dreamed –
                too soon – it had sounded.

A Rector's Memory

(ST ANDREWS, 1923)

The Gods that are wiser than Learning
    But kinder than Life have made sure
No mortal may boast in the morning
    That even will find him secure.
5 With naught for fresh faith or new trial,
    With little unsoiled or unsold,
Can the shadow go back on the dial,
    Or a new world be given for the old?
       But he knows not what time shall awaken,
10   *As he knows not what tide shall lay bare,*
       The heart of a man to be taken –
         Taken and changed unaware.

He shall see as he tenders his vows
    The far, guarded City arise –
15 The power of the North 'twixt her brows –
    The steel of the North in her eyes;
The sheer hosts of Heaven above –
    The grey warlock Ocean beside;
And shall feel the full centuries move
20   To Her purpose and pride.

Though a stranger shall he understand,
    As though it were old in his blood,
The lives that caught fire 'neath Her hand –
    The fires that were tamed to Her mood.
25 And the roar of the wind shall refashion,
    And the wind-driven torches recall,
The passing of Time and the passion
    Of Youth over all!
       And, by virtue of magic unspoken
30   *(What need She should utter Her power?)*
       The frost at his heart shall be broken
         And his spirit be changed in that hour –
          Changed and renewed in that hour!

Memories

1930

'The eradication of memories of the Great War.'

Socialist Government Organ

The Socialist Government speaks:

Though all the Dead were all forgot
    And razed were every tomb,
The Worm – the Worm that dieth not
    Compels Us to our doom.
5 Though all which once was England stands
    Subservient to Our will,
The Dead of whom we washed Our hands,
    They have observance still.

We laid no finger to Their load.
10   We multiplied Their woes.
We used Their dearly-opened road
    To traffic with Their foes:
And yet to Them men turn their eyes,
    To Them are vows renewed
15 Of Faith, Obedience, Sacrifice,
    Honour and Fortitude!

Which things must perish. But Our hour
    Comes not by staves or swords
So much as, subtly, through the power
20   Of small corroding words.
No need to make the plot more plain
    By any open thrust;
But – see Their memory is slain
    Long ere Their bones are dust!

25 Wisely, but yearly, filch some wreath –
    Lay some proud rite aside –
And daily tarnish with Our breath
    The ends for which They died.

Distract, deride, decry, confuse –
30   (Or – if it serve Us – pray!)
So presently We break the use
      And meaning of Their day!

Gertrude's Prayer

That which is marred at birth Time shall not mend,
      Nor water out of bitter well make clean;
All evil thing returneth at the end,
      Or elseway walketh in our blood unseen.
5 Whereby the more is sorrow in certaine –
Dayspring mishandled cometh not againe.

To-bruizèd be that slender, sterting spray
      Out of the oake's rind that should betide
A branch of girt and goodliness, straightway
10   Her spring is turnèd on herself, and wried
And knotted like some gall or veiney wen. –
Dayspring mishandled cometh not agen.

Noontide repayeth never morning-bliss –
      Sith noon to morn is incomparable;
15 And, so it be our dawning goth amiss,
      None other after-hour serveth well.
Ah! Jesu-Moder, pitie my oe paine –
Dayspring mishandled cometh not againe!

Four-Feet

I have done mostly what most men do,
And pushed it out of my mind;
But I can't forget, if I wanted to,
Four-Feet trotting behind.

5 Day after day, the whole day through –
  Wherever my road inclined –
  Four-Feet said, 'I am coming with you!'
  And trotted along behind.

  Now I must go by some other round, –
10 Which I shall never find –
  Somewhere that does not carry the sound
  Of Four-Feet trotting behind.

The Disciple

  He that hath a Gospel
    To loose upon Mankind,
  Though he serve it utterly –
    Body, soul and mind –
5 Though he go to Calvary
    Daily for its gain –
  It is His Disciple
    Shall make his labour vain.

  He that hath a Gospel
10   For all earth to own –
  Though he etch it on the steel,
    Or carve it on the stone –
  Not to be misdoubted
    Through the after-days –
15 It is His Disciple
    Shall read it many ways.

  It is His Disciple
    (Ere Those Bones are dust)
  Who shall change the Charter,
20   Who shall split the Trust –
  Amplify distinctions,
    Rationalize the Claim,
  Preaching that the Master
    Would have done the same.

25   It is His Disciple
         Who shall tell us how
     Much the Master would have scrapped
         Had he lived till now –
     What he would have modified
30   Of what he said before –
     It is His Disciple
         Shall do this and more . . .

     He that hath a Gospel
         Whereby Heaven is won
35   (Carpenter, or Cameleer,
         Or Maya's dreaming son),
     Many swords shall pierce Him,
         Mingling blood with gall;
     But His Own Disciple
40   Shall wound Him worst of all!

The Threshold

     In their deepest caverns of limestone
         They pictured the Gods of Food –
     The Horse, the Elk, and the Bison –
         That the hunting might be good;
5   With the Gods of Death and Terror –
         The Mammoth, Tiger, and Bear.
     And the pictures moved in the torchlight
         To show that the gods were there!
             But that was before Ionia –
10   (Or the Seven Holy Islands of Ionia)
             Any of the Mountains of Ionia,
             Had bared their peaks to the air.

     The close years packed behind them,
         As the glaciers bite and grind,
15   Filling the new-gouged valleys
         With Gods of every kind.

Gods of all-reaching power –
   Gods of all-searching eyes –
But each to be wooed by worship
20   And won by sacrifice.
        Till, after many winters, rose Ionia –
        (Strange men brooding in Ionia)
        Crystal-eyed Sages of Ionia
        Who said, 'These tales are lies.

25 We dream one Breath in all things,
     That blows all things between.
We dream one Matter in all things –
     Eternal, changeless, unseen.
That the heart of the Matter is single
30   Till the Breath shall bid it bring forth –
By choosing or losing its neighbour –
     All things made upon Earth.'
        But Earth was wiser than Ionia
        (Babylon and Egypt than Ionia)
        And they overlaid the teaching of Ionia
35   And the Truth was choked at birth.

It died at the Gate of Knowledge –
     The Key to the Gate in its hand –
And the anxious priests and wizards
40   Re-blinded the wakening land;
For they showed, by answering echoes,
     And chasing clouds as they rose,
How shadows should stand for bulwarks
     Between mankind and its woes.
45   It was then that men bethought them of Ionia
        (The few that had not allforgot Ionia)
        Or the Word that was whispered in Ionia;
        And they turned from the shadows and the shows.

They found one Breath in all things,
50   That moves all things between.
They proved one Matter in all things –
     Eternal, changeless, unseen;

That the heart of the Matter was single
 Till the Breath should bid it bring forth –
55   Even as men whispered in Ionia,
   (Resolute, unsatisfied Ionia)
   Ere the Word was stifled in Ionia –
  All things known upon earth!

The Expert

Youth that trafficked long with Death,
 And to second life returns,
Squanders little time or breath
 On his fellow-man's concerns.
5 Earnèd peace is all he asks
To fulfil his broken tasks.

Yet, if he find war at home
 (Waspish and importunate),
He hath means to overcome
10 Any warrior at his gate;
For the past he buried brings
Back unburiable things –

Nights that he lay out to spy
 Whence and when the raid might start;
15 Or prepared in secrecy
  Sudden blows to break its heart –
All the lore of No-Man's Land
Moves his soul and arms his hand.

So, if conflict vex his life
20 Where he thought all conflict done,
He, resuming ancient strife,
  Springs his mine or trains his gun,
And, in mirth more dread than wrath,
Wipes the nuisance from his path!

The Storm Cone

1932

This is the midnight – let no star
Delude us – dawn is very far.
This is the tempest long foretold –
Slow to make head but sure to hold.

5   Stand by! The lull 'twixt blast and blast
Signals the storm is near, not past;
And worse than present jeopardy
May our forlorn to-morrow be.

If we have cleared the expectant reef,
10   Let no man look for his relief.
Only the darkness hides the shape
Of further peril to escape.

It is decreed that we abide
The weight of gale against the tide
15   And those huge waves the outer main
Sends in to set us back again.

They fall and whelm. We strain to hear
The pulses of her labouring gear,
Till the deep throb beneath us proves,
20   After each shudder and check, she moves!

She moves, with all save purpose lost,
To make her offing from the coast;
But, till she fetches open sea,
Let no man deem that he is free!

The Bonfires

1933

'Gesture ... outlook ... vision ... avenue ... example ...
achievement ... appeasement ... limit of risk.'

Common Political Form

We know the Rocket's upward whizz;
    We know the Boom before the Bust.
We know the whistling Wail which is
    The Stick returning to the Dust.
5   We know how much to take on trust
Of any promised Paradise.
    We know the Pie – likewise the Crust.
We know the Bonfire on the Ice.

We know the Mountain and the Mouse.
10   We know Great Cry and Little Wool.
We know the purseless Ears of Sows.
    We know the Frog that aped the Bull.
    We know, whatever Trick we pull,
(Ourselves have gambled once or twice)
15   A Bobtailed Flush is not a Full
We know the Bonfire on the Ice.

We know that Ones and Ones make Twos –
    Till Demos votes them Three or Nought.
We know the Fenris Wolf is loose.
20   We know what Fight has not been fought.
    We know the Father to the Thought
Which argues Babe and Cockatrice
    Would play together, were they taught.
We know *that* Bonfire on the Ice.

25   We know that Thriving comes by Thrift.
    We know the Key must keep the Door.
We know his Boot-straps cannot lift
    The frightened Waster off the Floor.

We know these things, and we deplore
30   That not by any Artifice
Can they be altered. Furthermore
We know the Bonfires on the Ice!

The Appeal

If I have given you delight
By aught that I have done,
Let me lie quiet in that night
Which shall be yours anon:

5   And for the little, little, span
The dead are borne in mind,
Seek not to question other than
The books I leave behind.

Notes

The title of each poem is followed by details of the poem's first publication, and then, where applicable, by the title of the volume in which it was subsequently collected.

'We are very slightly changed' (p. 1). The opening poem of *Departmental Ditties* (1886) with the title 'General Summary'. As it also serves here as the opening poem, it is placed slightly out of chronology. The reference to 'Dowb' (line 7) is obscure, perhaps a Kipling joke ('Director of Works and Buildings'). Line 23, Cheops, King of Egypt, 2900–2877 BC; lines 26–9, Joseph . . . Pharaoh, Genesis 41.

'The Undertaker's Horse' (p. 2). *Civil and Military Gazette*, 8 October 1885; *Departmental Ditties*. Line 22, *dâk*, stage of a journey; line 36, marigolds, used in India to decorate graves.

'The Story of Uriah' (p. 4). *Civil and Military Gazette*, 3 March 1886; *Departmental Ditties*. An updated version of the story of David and Bathsheba, as the biblical reference indicates. Simla (line 3), a hill-station in the lower Himalayas, the summer residence of the Viceroy and the imperial government, and a favoured holiday resort for officials' wives. It was famed for its cool climate, unlike Quetta (line 1), the town in what is now Pakistan to which Jack Barrett is sent. The Hurnai (line 26), a mountain pass in Afghanistan.

'Public Waste' (p. 5). *Civil and Military Gazette*, 9 March 1886; *Departmental Ditties*. Line 1, Sir Robert Walpole, eighteenth-century British Prime Minister; line 6, the Viceroy and the imperial administration at Simla; line 7, Kipling's own 'family circle'; line 8, Chatham, in Kent, where the School of Military Engineering was based; line 17, Vauban, a French military engineer of the seventeenth century, famed for his theories of fortification; line 18, the Staff College, Camberley; line 25, an, if, archaism used several times by Kipling in his early poems; line 27, Fifty and Five, the age of retirement; line 31, Bhamo, a district in Upper Burma.

'The Plea of the Simla Dancers' (p. 6). *Civil and Military Gazette*, 16 April 1886; *Departmental Ditties*. Benmore (line 8), a popular club and dance hall in Simla, closed to make more office space, an event marked by Kipling with this unusually elegant mock-heroic complaint. Line 3, swept and garnished, Matthew 12:44; line 9, *duftar*, an office; line 11, Babus, English-speaking Bengali clerks; line 14, Strawberry Hill, a private house in Simla, formerly offices.

'The Lovers' Litany' (p. 8). *Departmental Ditties*. Litany is a form of public prayer in which the clergy lead and the congregation responds, though secularized here. Line 13, the Southern Cross, a constellation in the shape of a cross given sentimental significance by travellers as indicating movement from the southern to the northern hemisphere, or vice versa. In this instance it represents nostalgia for home.

'The Overland Mail' (p. 9). *Departmental Ditties* (2nd ed., 1886). Called originally 'Her Majesty's Mail', it may have been an influence on W.H. Auden's very similar rhythmic poem 'Night Mail' (1935).

'Christmas in India' (p. 10). *Pioneer*, 24 December 1886; *Departmental Ditties* (3rd ed., 1888). Homesickness was a common experience of many generations of the British overseas, civilians and military, and Kipling often writes about it. The speaker in this poem is doubly exiled, from Christmas festivities at home and from the very different religious observances going on around him in India. Line 1, tamarisks, small evergreen trees; line 12, ghat, a landing place, quay; line 13, Rama, mythological hero of a Sanskrit epic; line 21, *Heimweh*, German for homesickness.

'Look, you have cast out Love!' (p. 12). Epigraph to 'Lispeth', *Plain Tales from the Hills* (1888); *Songs from Books* (1913) Originally with the ironic title 'The Convert'. Line 6, probably an allusion to Swinburne's anti-Christian poem 'Hymn to Proserpine' (1866).

'A stone's throw out on either hand' (p. 12). Epigraph to 'In the House of Suddhoo', *Plain Tales from the Hills*; *Songs from Books*. Originally called 'From the Dusk to the Dawn'. The supernatural element in this particular story turns out to be fraudulent, but the poem expresses a serious and lifelong concern of Kipling's. Line 4, *Churel*, the ghost of a woman who has died in childbirth; ghoul, an evil spirit that preys on the dead; djinn, a spirit capable of assuming human form.

'The Betrothed' (p. 13). *Pioneer*, 21 November 1888; *Departmental Ditties* (4th ed., 1890). In the *Sussex Edition* the breach of promise case is identified as having taken place in Glasgow. Kipling, however, was drawing on a well-established theme of light verse and music-hall songs in which a confirmed bachelor rejects promised domestic bliss for the more reliable contentment provided by his cigar or pipe. Line 28, *Suttee*, the rite of widow-burning; line 49, the fact that the population of Britain contained more women than men was a major concern of Victorian social commentators. These women were described as 'surplus' and urged to emigrate in order to find husbands.

'The Winners' (p. 16). Published originally as 'L'Envoi' to *The Story of the Gadsbys* (1888); with the present title, *Songs from Books*. It contains echoes of several poems by Robert Browning. Line 5, Gehenna, a place of suffering and torment, 'Hell'.

'I have eaten your bread and salt' (p. 16). A dedicatory poem, 'Prelude', written for the 4th edition of *Departmental Ditties* (1890), by which time Kipling had left India and was pursuing his career in London, hence the retrospective tone of the poem. In the *Definitive Edition* it is dated 1885. Line 1, bread and salt, the ancient ritual of hospitality offered and accepted; line 10, sheltered people, the English in England.

'Danny Deever' (p. 17). *Scots Observer*, 22 February 1890; *Barrack-Room Ballads* (1892). A question-and-answer ballad between the ordinary soldiers ('Files-on-Parade') and their Colour-Sergeant (responsible for attending the regimental colours on an occasion such as this). It is often claimed that Kipling was drawing on literary sources from earlier in the nineteenth century for this event, but military executions of the kind described here did take place in India in the 1880s. Line 6, 'ollow square, three sides of a square with the soldiers facing inwards; line 7, the buttons, stripes and regimental markings on Danny Deever's uniform are roughly torn off to indicate the disgrace he has brought on the regiment.

'Tommy' (p. 18). *Scots Observer*, 1 March 1890; *Barrack-Room Ballads*. Thomas Atkins (and subsequently 'Tommy' applied to any private soldier in the British army) was originally the specimen or type name for use in army documentation. It is said to have been chosen by the Duke of Wellington. The great popularity of the name dates, however, from this poem which robustly defends 'Tommy' against civilian hypocrisy. Line 19, goin' large a bit, being noisy or rowdy; line 22, 'Thin red line of 'eroes', advancing into battle in a 'thin' line, the soldiers dramatically identified by their scarlet tunics.

'Private Ortheris's Song' (p. 20). Sung by Ortheris (one of the 'soldiers three') at the close of the story 'The Courting of Dinah Shadd', *Macmillan's Magazine*, March 1890; *Life's Handicap* (1891). It was not included in *Barrack-Room Ballads*. Line 1, onest (in some editions 'onst'), once; line 5, acceptance of the Queen's shilling marked the agreement of a civilian to join the army; line 18, *dah*, a short sword; line 26, pop, slang for champagne, though here presumably a humbler form of alcohol; line 28, 'shop', guard-house; line 31, C.B., confined to barracks.

'Soldier, Soldier' (p. 22). *Scots Observer*, 12 April 1890; *Barrack-Room Ballads*. Line 11, the 'suit o' rifle-green' identifies the dead soldier as a member of a 'rifle regiment', trained to act as a scout and sharp-shooter.

'The Widow at Windsor' (p. 23). *Scots Observer*, 26 April 1890, with the title 'The Sons of the Widow'; *Barrack-Room Ballads*. Many of the early barrack-room ballads show the speakers as angry, cynical or disillusioned, and nowhere more so than here. Line 1, the Widow, Queen Victoria; line 2, hairy, a euphemism for 'bloody' or similar adjective; line 4, beggars, euphemism for 'buggers'; line 6, nick, army troop horses were marked and numbered on the near forefoot; line 28, Lodge ... tile, the speaker, like Kipling himself, is obviously a freemason: the movement was strong in India. A Lodge is a masonic 'workshop' and to 'tile' it is to protect it from intruders. It is compared favourably with the Widow's Lodge (i.e. the British Empire); line 36, Wings o' the Mornin', Psalms 139:9; line 39, bloomin' old rag, the British flag.

'Gunga Din' (p. 25). *Scots Observer*, 7 June 1890; *Barrack-Room Ballads*. Based on the true story of Juma, water-carrier with the 'Guides' at the siege of Delhi, 1857. In recognition of his bravery in action the men of the Guides petitioned that he be allowed to join them. He was also awarded a medal 'For Valour'. The poem is best seen as a dramatic recitation of the kind very popular in music hall. Line 3, penny-fights, frontier skirmishes. Aldershot, the army training camp in Hampshire, here turned into a scornful verb (i.e. to spend time training rather than fighting); line 12, *bhisti*, water-carrier; lines 15–16, *hitherao panee lao*, bring water quickly; line 27, *Harry By*, Oh brother; line 32, *juldee*, be quick; line 33, *marrow*, hit; line 41, *mussick*, leather water-bag; line 70, dooli, canvas litter; line 77, drills, drill prior to *Sussex*.

'Mandalay' (p. 27). *Scots Observer*, 21 June 1890; *Barrack-Room Ballads*. As in 'Christmas in India' the experience evoked is one of nostalgia, but for an adopted rather than a natural home (line 30), a theme frequently explored by Kipling. He visited Burma briefly in 1889 when the country was regarded as part of British India: his journey is described in *From Sea to Sea* (2 vols, 1900), where many of the details in the poem are to be found. Line 1, 'lookin lazy at the sea' in *Definitive Edition*. Mulmein is in the south of the country, Mandalay in the centre; line 6, the paddle-steamers of the Irrawaddy Flotilla Company; line 12, King Theebaw and Queen Supaya-lat, rulers of Upper Burma, driven into exile by the British in 1885; line 22, *hathis*, elephants; line 24, squdgy, Kipling's coinage.

'The Young British Soldier' (p. 29). *Scots Observer*, 28 June 1890; *Barrack-Room Ballads*. The speaker is an experienced soldier, perhaps a training sergeant, giving advice to young recruits about to be sent ('drafted', line 9) to India. Line 10, rag-box, used to hold cleaning materials, and also mouth ('rag', slang for tongue); line 29, fatigues, tedious jobs, often dispensed as light punishments; line 50, Martini-Henry, a high-velocity breech-loading rifle used by the army in the 1880s; line 56, limbers, the detachable frame of a gun carriage; line 61, take open order, spread out.

'The Conundrum of the Workshops' (p. 31). *Scots Observer*, 13 September 1890; *Barrack-Room Ballads*. An earlier version called 'New Lamps for Old' is included in Rutherford's *Early Verse*, p. 445. The biblical references (Adam and Eve, the Flood, the Tower of Babel, the Serpent in the Garden) are from Genesis. Line 22, yelk, yolk. Line 25 brings the perennial debate on 'What is Art?' up to date by placing it in London's clubland, without getting any nearer to an answer.

'Ford o' Kabul River' (p. 33). *National Observer*, 22 November 1890; *Barrack-Room Ballads*. Based on an incident involving British cavalry during an advance in 1879 on Kabul, the capital of Afghanistan. Kipling heightens the night-time chaos when horses and men were swept away in the river by focusing on the distress felt by just one soldier at the loss of a comrade. In the *Definitive Edition*, the second line of each stanza has 'trumpet' instead of 'bugle'.

'The English Flag' (p. 35). *National Observer*, 4 April 1891; *Barrack-Room Ballads*. This poem marks Kipling's emergence as a spokesman for the British Empire, with the swinging aggressive verse urging the British people to imperial service and, at the same time, denouncing the anti-imperialists (lines 2-3, 54). The Four Winds are called to testify to the spread of the Empire throughout the world. The boastful tone provoked a critical hostility that Kipling was never to shake off, while supporters of British expansion hailed the courage, daring, and exhilaration that the poem also celebrates. The report in 'Daily Papers' that provides the poem's starting point concerned a demonstration on 27 March 1891, during a trial of Irish political agitators, when the court-house at Cork was set on fire. Line 10, Disko, an island off Greenland; line 23, sea-egg, a vividly-coloured sea urchin; line 29, halliards, ropes used to hoist sails; line 37, the Kuriles, chain of volcanic islands in the North Pacific; line 40, Praya, a wharf; line 43, Hugli ('Hoogli' in the *Definitive Edition*), the river on which Calcutta stands; line 61, wrack-wreath, dangerous shipwreck weather.

'The beasts are very wise' (p. 38). One of several short poems written for the book *Beast and Man in India* (1891) by John Lockwood Kipling; *Songs from Books*.

'Cells' (p. 39). *Barrack-Room Ballads*. Line 1, button-stick, a piece of slotted metal used to hold tunic buttons away from the cloth while cleaning them; line 7, pack-drill, marching up-and-down in full order; C.B., confined to barracks; line 19, stripes, awarded for good conduct.

'The Widow's Party' (p. 40). *Barrack-Room Ballads*. Line 3, lay, job; line 6, Gosport Hard, naval depôt at Portsmouth; line 18, knives and forks, swords and bayonets; line 26, mess, a group of soldiers eating meals together.

'The Exiles' Line' (p. 42). *Civil and Military Gazette*, 8 July 1892. In the *Definitive Edition* it is dated 1890, perhaps indicating the date of composition; or, it may be Kipling looking back in a melancholy mood on the India he had recently left. The luxurious ships of the P. & O. (the Peninsular and Oriental Steam Navigation Company) carry the 'exiles' to and fro, and are presented as a microcosm of British India: even the classical Fates have little power on a P. & O. steamer (lines 37-8). Line 3, Blue Peter, the signal that a ship is ready to sail; line 5, Coupons, obscure, but possibly pre-paid ticket holders, or non-passengers who must now leave the ship; line 6, Grindlay, publisher of travel books for visitors to India; line 7, Gardafui, the eastern horn of Africa (now Somalia); line 51, Quartered Flag, of the P. & O. (red, white, blue, and yellow).

'When Earth's Last Picture is Painted' (p. 44). *New York Sun*, 28 August 1892, with the article 'Half-a-Dozen Pictures'; revised as 'L'Envoi' to *The Seven Seas* (1896). In the article, collected in *Letters of Travel* (1920), Kipling argues that the work of most painters is disappointing when compared with the real 'pictures' to be seen everywhere in the world itself. This view is closely related to that expressed in Robert Browning's poem 'Fra Lippo Lippi' (1855).

'In the Neolithic Age' (p. 45). First published, in part, with the article 'My First Book', *The Idler*, December 1892; in full, *The Seven Seas*. As elsewhere, an insistence that artistic problems are at least as old as the New Stone Age, and Art itself of many different varieties. Line 9, Solutré, an area in France with caves containing Stone Age relics; line 17, Totem, a venerated object; line 24, H.D.

Traill, a late Victorian critic involved in the debate on who should succeed Tennyson as Poet Laureate. He listed fifty possible contemporary poets for the post, and added the young Kipling's name as an after-thought; line 27, Allobrogenses, an ancient tribe in Gaul; amanuenses, scribes; line 28, prehistoric inhabitants of Switzerland living in raised lake-side huts; lines 35–6, Khatmandhu, the capital of Nepal; Clapham, the London base of the Evangelical sect; Martaban, a town near Moulmein in Burma (where, according to 'Mandalay', there 'aren't no Ten Commandments an' a man can raise a thirst').

'The Last Chantey' (p. 47). *Pall Mall Magazine*, 15 June 1893; *The Seven Seas*. Chantey/shanty, a song of the sea. Revelation 21:1 presents a vision of a new heaven and a new earth with no sea. Kipling goes back a stage and allows the various people who have loved the sea to beg God for a reprieve. Line 10, barracout', the voracious barracuda fish; line 27, picaroon, pirate ship; line 32, frap, to pass cables around a ship to save it breaking up from the weight of the sea; line 46, Gothavn, in Greenland, a centre of the whaling industry; line 47, flenching, cutting up whale blubber; line 48, ice-blink, a shimmer in the air caused by the reflection of ice; line 49, bowhead, a species of whale; line 54, Revelation 4:6; line 62, spindrift, sea spray.

'For to Admire' (p. 49). *Pall Mall Magazine*, February 1894; *The Seven Seas*. Line 8, Lascar, an East Indian sailor; *Hum deckty hai*, I'm looking out. Line 43, time-expired, with his military service completed.

'The Law of the Jungle' (p. 51). First published as 'The Law for the Wolves' with the story 'How Fear Came', *Pall Mall Budget*, 7 June 1894; *The Second Jungle Book* (1895); *Songs from Books*. In *The Second Jungle Book* these 'laws', or 'rulings', as Kipling also calls them, are 'always recited' by Baloo the Bear 'in a sort of sing-song'. Hathi (line 10) is the Elephant.

'The Three-Decker' (p. 54). *Saturday Review*, 14 July 1894; *The Seven Seas*. Most Victorian novels were first published in three large expensive volumes, known popularly as 'three-deckers' after the triple-tiered battleships. Readers would borrow the novels from circulating libraries rather than buy them. On 27 June 1894 the libraries renounced the system and it immediately collapsed. Like many of Kipling's poems, 'The Three-Decker' was, therefore, very topical. The literary and social conventions of the three-decker are treated affectionately, though now out-moded, as obsolete as the old sailing ships in an age of steam. Line 4, Islands of the Blest, Hesperides, the fabled gardens of Greek mythology; line 9, Cook, Thomas Cook the travel agent; line 16, Genesis 39, Zuleika (according to non-biblical sources) was the wife of Potiphar who tempted Joseph or 'Yussuf' which was also a *nom-de-plume* used by the young Kipling; line 27, However, howe'er so prior to *Sussex*; line 28, 'a ram-you-damn-you liner' was a passenger steamer concerned only with reaching its destination on time and careless with other smaller ships; line 31, in bad weather oil-bags were hung overboard to help ease the swell of the sea; line 33, threshing, beating against the wind; line 34, drogue, a temporary sea-anchor made of wooden planks; line 35, from truck to taffrail, adorned with flags the full length of the ropes holding the sails; line 45, crew, crews prior to *Sussex*.

'Back to the Army Again' (p. 56). *Pall Mall Magazine*, August 1894; *The Seven Seas*, where it was placed first in a new series of 'barrack-room ballads'. The speaker is a reservist, unsuccessful in civilian life, who changes his name and re-enlists illegally: his training sergeant connives at the subterfuge. At the close of the poem Kipling is urging the British government to treat soldiers more sensibly and to build up the regular army. Line 1, ticky ulster, lousy overcoat; billycock, a bowler; line 4, goose-step, an elementary drill exercise; line 28, rookies, new recruits; line 41, slops, his new uniform; line 49, swagger-cane, carried by all soldiers when in uniform in public.

'Road-Song of the *Bandar-Log*' (p. 58). Closing poem to the story 'Kaa's Hunting', *The Jungle Book* (1894). The *bandar-log* are monkeys, and in the jungle hierarchy outside 'the law'. They are feckless, given entirely to fun, untrustworthy, constantly changing and moving – qualities skilfully reflected in the poem's rhythms. Line 31, to scumfish, a Kipling coinage – skim/flying fish/scum. The monkeys may skim through the air like flying fish, but they are more truly allied with the scum on the water.

'McAndrew's Hymn' (p. 59). *Scribner's Magazine*, December 1894; *The Seven Seas*. In some editions the speaker's name is given the alternative form of M'Andrew, though Kipling settled finally on the present spelling. Two changes made for the *Sussex Edition* have been adopted here: 'wasna' for 'was not' (line 50) and 'fetish' for 'fetich' (line 66). The voyage from which McAndrew is returning is usually assumed to have been based on the one that Kipling himself took, from England to New Zealand via Cape Town, in 1891. The date of McAndrew's voyage, however, is fixed as 1887 by his reference to the death of his wife and the burning of the *Sarah Sands* taking place in the same year, 'thirty years ago' (lines 18–19). The *Sarah Sands* caught fire while carrying troops to India in 1857: Kipling wrote about the event and the 'undefeatable courage and cool-headedness' of the troops in *Land and Sea Tales for Scouts and Guides* (1923). 'McAndrew's Hymn' marks a change of direction in Kipling's work in the early 1890s, with his poems and stories beginning to focus more on the sea and seamen than on the army and soldiers. He was fascinated by naval technology and how its language could be used in poetry, and shared McAndrew's wish that modern poets would learn 'to sing the Song o' Steam' (line 151). McAndrew's visionary experience at sea leads him to reject his harsh Calvinist upbringing in Glasgow (lines 59–70) for a new religion of machinery and, more tentatively, of 'Man – the Arrtifex', the artificer (line 177). This becomes his 'Institutio' (line 6), a reference to Calvin's statement of Protestant belief in *Institutio Christianae Religionis* (1536). There are, however, indications that McAndrew remains influenced by Calvinism: he insists that he is not yet a follower of Pelagius (line 186), who believed that salvation was a matter of free will rather than predestination, and the qualities demanded by McAndrew's new religion (line 167) are unremittingly stern.

'The Men that fought at Minden' (p. 67). *Pall Mall Gazette*, 9 May 1895; *The Seven Seas*. Minden, a battle in 1759 in the Seven Years War when the French cavalry were defeated by British infantry. The Lodge of the subtitle suggests a masonic meaning, though the poem shouldn't be taken too straightforwardly. The instructor is ill-informed and full of bluster: ultimately he is concerned with getting the new recruits to buy him drinks. Line 3, Maiwand, a British military defeat in Afghanistan, 1880; line 9, stocks, supports; line 16, club, to bunch together while marching; line 21, musketoons, heavy large-bore guns; line 22, halberdiers were soldiers armed with 'halberts' or pikes; line 44, Johnny Raw, a new recruit.

'The stream is shrunk – the pool is dry' (p. 69). Opening poem to the story 'How Fear Came', *The Second Jungle Book*; *Songs from Books*.

'The 'Eathen' (p. 70). *McClure's Magazine*, September 1896; *The Seven Seas*. The first line is taken from a hymn written by Bishop Heber, 'From Greenland's Icy Mountains' (1821), which Kipling alludes to at various points in his work. The hymn exhorts missionaries to deliver 'the heathen' from spiritual darkness. Kipling's point is that everyone (the soldier in particular) is saved by discipline and order rather than by religion. Lines 7, 23, 75, '*abby-nay*', not now; '*kul*', tomorrow; and '*hazar-ho*', wait a bit, were pidgin-Hindustani words commonly used by British soldiers in India. Line 62, dooli, canvas litter.

'The King' (p. 73). Published, in part, with the title 'Romance' in *Under Lochnagar*, edited by R.A. Profeit (Aberdeen, 1894); in full, with the present title, *The Seven Seas*. Line 16, arquebus and culverin, early guns; line 24, refers to the charting of prevailing winds; line 34, 'local' instead of 'agent' in *The Seven Seas* and *Definitive Edition*, changed for the *Sussex*; line 40, the reeking Banks, of Newfoundland.

'The Derelict' (p. 74). *The Seven Seas*. One of many poems and stories written in the mid 1890s in which Kipling takes an anthropomorphic approach to ships and machinery. Line 9, con, to direct or control; line 14, wried, contorted; line 23, hawse-pipes, the holes in a ship's bows through which the anchor-cable passes; line 36, comber, a large curling wave; line 37, careen, to lean on one side; line 42, strake, a plank or plate in the side of a ship.

'When 'Omer smote 'is bloomin' lyre' (p. 76). Prelude to the 'barrack-room ballads' section of *The Seven Seas*.

'The Ladies' (p. 76). The famous final stanza was used as an epigraph to 'The Courting of Dinah Shadd', *Macmillan's Magazine*, March 1890, and in *Life's Handicap* (1891). In full in the 'barrack-room ballads' section of *The Seven Seas*. Like 'Gunga Din' the poem is closer to a music-hall recitation than a ballad, in that it demands to be acted out in character. The various towns and countries mentioned chart the speaker's army postings as well as his sexual relationships: Prome (Burma), 'Oogli (Calcutta), Neemuch (Rajasthan, India), Mhow (central India), Meerut (near Delhi). Line 7, *jemadar-sais*, head-groom; line 26, acting-sergeant in charge of the regimental canteen; line 37, *bolee*, slang.

'The Sergeant's Weddin'' (p. 78). One of the 'barrack-room ballads' in *The Seven Seas*. Line 11, the horses and the smart 'lando' (landau) indicate the Sergeant's pretentiousness; line 12, etc., to avoid the obvious rhyming word whore; line 16, keeps canteen, a notorious way of making money out of the soldiers and one of the reasons why they have 'scores to settle' (line 25); line 33, side-arms, bayonets carried on the belt.

'The Vampire' (p. 80). Not collected until *Inclusive Edition* (1919). Written to accompany a painting of the same name by Kipling's cousin, Philip Burne-Jones, and published in the catalogue of an exhibition at the New Gallery, London, and in the *Daily Mail*, 17 April 1897. Bram Stoker's novel *Dracula* was published in June of the same year.

'Recessional' (p. 81). *The Times*, 17 July 1897; *The Five Nations* (1903). Written to mark Queen Victoria's Diamond Jubilee, though published nearly a month after the main celebrations, it astonished both admirers and critics of Kipling's work by its solemn tone and its warning that the British Empire could well follow the fate of others, like Nineveh and Tyre (line 16), if it was not nurtured in a mood of humility. The poem is built on a series of biblical allusions and echoes, the most central being Deuteronomy 6:10–15. Lines 21–2, 'Gentiles ... lesser breeds without the Law', controversial and much-debated lines, drawn from Paul's Epistle to the Romans 2:8–14.

'The White Man's Burden' (p. 82). *The Times*, 4 February 1899; *The Five Nations*. The poem was first headed 'An Address to America', and the explanatory subtitle added only for the *Definitive Edition*. After the brief war between America and Spain in 1898, responsibility for administering the Philippines and Cuba was taken over by America, until then a leading anti-imperialist country and often a stern critic of the British Empire. Kipling welcomed this apparent change of policy and is urging America to join in a worldwide campaign. The poem emphasizes service rather than conquest, but even so his enthusiasm allows him to give expression to a mood of white superiority which is not usually characteristic of his work. Lines 39–40, Exodus 16:2–3.

'Cruisers' (p. 84). *Morning Post*, 14 August 1899; revised for *The Five Nations*. The traditional job of the cruiser (formerly carried out by the frigate) was to seek out enemy ships and lure them into battle, hence Kipling's extended comparison of them with sea-port prostitutes. Line 29, spindrift, spray from waves; line 35, widdershins, anti-clockwise; line 37, levin, a flash of lightning.

'A School Song' (p. 86). Introductory poem to *Stalky & Co*. (1899), a collection of fictionalized stories based on Kipling's schooldays at the United Services College, Westward Ho!; *Songs from Books*. The first line is taken from *The Apocrypha*, Ecclesiasticus 44: 'Let us now praise famous men, and our fathers that begat us.'

'The Absent-Minded Beggar' (p. 88). *Daily Mail*, 31 October 1899 and in many different popular forms to raise money for the wives and children of soldiers serving in the Boer War (1899–1902). Not collected until *Inclusive Edition* (1919). As in the soldier ballads 'beggar' is a euphemism for 'bugger' and would have been widely accepted as such at the time. Line 2, Paul Kruger, President of the Transvaal, a Boer leader much parodied in popular British songs and cartoons; line 22, a reference to a very popular soldiers' song, 'The girl I left behind me', though the words of the song were often more cynical than they are here.

'The Two-Sided Man' (p. 90). The opening two stanzas first published as an epigraph to Chapter 8 of *Kim* (1901); enlarged and revised for *Songs from Books*. In its original setting the dichotomy is between English and Indian ways of life, though its wider personal meaning refers to the many apparently conflicting aspects of Kipling's life and art. Lines 11–12, holy figures representing the variety of religious beliefs in the world: Shaman (Asiatic Russian), Ju-ju (African), Angekok (Eskimo), Mukamuk (Red Indian), Bonze (Buddhist).

'Bridge-Guard in the Karroo' (p. 91). *The Times*, 5 June 1901; *The Five Nations*. The Karroo, a bleak plateau between Cape Town and Johannesburg, where 'details' (men 'detailed' to the job) are guarding the Blood River railway bridge. Line 3, Oudtshoorn, mountains in Cape Colony; line 7, beryl, pale-green; line 15, picket, a group of men set to protect a specific place; line 22, ganger, a foreman in charge of workers; line 29, Hottentot, native South African.

'The Lesson' (p. 93). *The Times*, 29 July 1901; *The Five Nations*. Kipling was fundamentally affected by the difficulties the British army experienced in the Boer War and, subsequently, what he regarded as the betrayal of South Africa by the British government, especially the Liberals who came to power in 1905. This jaunty poem, with its heavy rhymes, sarcasm, and refrain adapted from Gilbert and Sullivan's *Trial by Jury* (1875) – 'It was managed by a job, and a good job too' – was one immediate response as the war was drawing to an end. Other, very different poetic responses, were to follow. Line 5, the phrase means to be punished excessively; line 9, the South African place names mark the boundaries of the war area; lines 16–17, it took a long time for the Commanders of the British army to realize that in South African conditions fast-moving horsemen were more effective troops than infantry; line 24, Rand, the gold-mining area, and the unit of currency, of South Africa.

'The Islanders' (p. 95). *The Times*, 4 January 1902; *The Five Nations*. One conviction Kipling drew from the Boer War was that Britain needed to prepare militarily for a larger war in the future that would be provoked by Germany. His belief in some form of military conscription was not shared by most people in Britain, and in this poem he attacked the ruling classes for being committed more to their own narrow tribal customs than to Britain's safety. Line 1, Job 12:2; line 15, 'hampered and hindered' in editions earlier than the *Sussex*; line 76, Baals, false gods; line 77, Teraphs of sept, idols of a tribe or clan.

'The Camel's hump is an ugly lump' (p. 99). Follows the story 'How the Camel Got His Hump', *Just So Stories* (1902); *Songs from Books*.

'I keep six honest serving-men' (p. 100). Follows the story 'The Elephant's Child,' *Just So Stories*; *Songs from Books*.

'I've never sailed the Amazon' (p. 100). Follows the story 'The Beginning of the Armadilloes', *Just So Stories*; *Songs from Books*. The poem expresses a personal wish of Kipling's to 'roll down to Rio' which was realized much later in his life, a journey described in *Brazilian Sketches* (1927).

'Pussy can sit by the fire and sing' (p. 101). Follows the story 'The Cat that Walked by Himself', *Just So Stories*; *Songs from Books*.

'The Settler' (p. 102). *The Times*, 27 February 1903; *The Five Nations*. Published almost a year after the end of the Boer War, the tone is notably more one of reconciliation than in the earlier poems. Line 21, murrain, pestilence; lines 39–40, 'But Jesus saith unto him, Follow me; and leave the dead to bury their own dead', Matthew 8:22.

'Before a midnight breaks in storm' (p. 104). Written as the introductory poem, the 'Dedication', of *The Five Nations*, it reveals Kipling as a prophet of disaster to come, unless the signs are truly understood and acted upon. Lines 35–6, wingèd men . . . Fates, at this time the first successful aeroplane flights were being carried out and Kipling realized they would transform the nature of war. There may also be a play on the winged Harpies, the avenging monsters of Greek mythology.

'The Second Voyage' (p. 105). *The Five Nations*. This obscure allegory is usually seen as a light-hearted skit on youthful love, though perhaps it belongs more suitably to the darker prophetic side of *The Five Nations*, with the 'little Cupids' being put ashore if they are unwilling to confront the 'foul weather' that is to come. Line 9, remede, remedy; line 13, petrels, birds whose presence near a ship foretells stormy weather; line 21, Paphos, a town in Cyprus dedicated to Aphrodite, the goddess of love; Line 37, warp, to haul a ship into deep water before raising the sails; line 39, Hesperides, the blessed islands of Greek mythology.

'The Broken Men' (p. 106). *The Five Nations*. Callao (line 16), a port in Peru, was at this time a haven for men wanted by the British Law. T.S. Eliot acknowledged the influence of the title on that of his own poem 'The Hollow Men', and the final lines suggest that Rupert Brooke was also influenced by it at the close of 'The Old Vicarage, Grantchester'. Line 37, yucca, a South American plant with sword-shaped leaves; line 40, jalousies, slatted window-blinds; line 71, Lord Warden, a hotel at Dover, named after the Lord Warden of the Cinque Ports on the south coast of England.

'Sussex' (p. 108). *The Five Nations*. Bateman's, at Burwash in Sussex, became the Kipling family home in 1902. From now on the county of Sussex was to provide the setting for many of his stories and poems. Line 8, Genesis 1:31; line 12, Levuka's Trade, the trade wind that sweeps Levuka, one of the Fiji Islands; line 14, *Book of Common Prayer*, Psalms 16:7; line 43, dewpond, a small reservoir; line 55, Wilfrid, patron saint of Sussex; line 67, a giant chalk figure built into the hillside; line 73, shaws, thickets or groves; line 74, ghylls, rocky clefts in hills; lines 77–8, Piddinghoe, a village near Newhaven; the 'begilded dolphin' refers to the weather vane on the village church.

'Dirge of Dead Sisters' (p. 111). *The Five Nations*. Line 11, culvert, a conduit carrying water; line 28, 'Mine eyes have seen the glory of the coming of the Lord', *Battle Hymn of the Republic*; line 35, Uitvlugt, hospital and isolation camp for plague victims, Cape Town; line 36, Mary Kingsley, explorer and writer, known to Kipling before the war, volunteered to serve as a nursing sister at Simon's Town (a naval dockyard), where she died looking after Boer prisoners.

'Chant-Pagan' (p. 113). *The Five Nations*. In Latin, *paganus* was a villager or rustic, liable to be enrolled in the army, though of inferior status to the professional soldier (*miles*). The speaker in this poem has served as an 'Irregular' in the Boer War and now, bored with the inferior position allotted him in the social life of an English village, decides to emigrate to South Africa. Line 13, kopje, hill; kop, mountain; line 15, 'elios, heliographs, instruments for communicating signals by reflected sunlight; line 24, Ma'ollisberg Range, Magaliesberg, mountains near Johannesburg; lines 35–40, place-names of military engagements in the Boer War; line 58, Vaal . . . Orange, the names of rivers in South Africa.

'Lichtenberg' (p. 116). *The Five Nations*. Lichtenberg, a town in the Transvaal. Kipling was greatly impressed by the support given to Britain by the Dominions in the Boer War. The evocative refrain of the poem is reputed to have come from the actual words of an Australian soldier overheard by Kipling. Line 7, wattle, Acacia (mimosa), the Australian national flower.

'Stellenbosch' (p. 117). *The Five Nations*. Stellenbosch was a British base camp near Cape Town to which incompetent officers were transferred; they were 'stellenbosched', as the process came to be known. The term is now obsolete, though Kipling's phrase for 'a cover-up' (lines 9–10) is still current. Throughout his life, Kipling speaks on behalf of the ordinary soldier and against corrupt or incompetent administration, as in this instance where the generals are more concerned with the knighthoods and medals they might receive (lines 38–41) than with prosecuting the war energetically. Sub-title, Composite Columns, the combined military forces operating against the Boers; line 11, sugared about, euphemistic for 'buggered about'; line 21, Boojers, burghers, Dutch 'citizens'; line 22, bandolier, a belt carrying ammunition; line 24, stoep, the wooden verandah of Dutch-style houses; line 30, Christiaan De Wet, Boer Commander; line 35, pompom, light automatic gun; line 37, kranzes, cliffs.

'Harp Song of the Dane Women' (p. 119). Introductory poem to story 'The Knights of the Joyous Venture', *Puck of Pook's Hill* (1906); *Songs from Books*.

'Rimini' (p. 120). First stanza in the story 'On the Great Wall', *Strand Magazine*, June 1906, and *Puck of Pook's Hill*; expanded for *Songs from Books*. Described in the story as a popular Roman soldiers' marching song, it is a variation on 'The girl I left behind me', which Kipling refers to in several of his barrack-room ballads. 'Later' Roman Empire indicated by the soldiers being fed up with military campaigns and eager to get home. The name Lalage is taken from Horace. Rimini, a town on the Adriatic coast. Line 7, Pontic, the Black Sea; line 13, Via Aurelia, the coast road from Rome to Genoa and then on to Gaul (France); line 31, Narbo, Narbonne in southern France, site of the first Roman colony in Gaul; line 35, Eagles, the Roman military insignia, and hence the soldiers themselves.

'Prophets at Home' (p. 121). Opening poem to the story 'Hal o' the Draft', *Puck of Pook's Hill*; *Songs from Books*. Second stanza, Jonah 4.

'A Smuggler's Song' (p. 121). Closing poem to the story 'Hal o' the Draft', *Puck of Pook's Hill*; *Songs from Books*. Line 19, George III; line 29, Valenciennes, French lace.

'The Sons of Martha' (p. 123). *The Standard*, 29 April 1907; *The Years Between* (1919). The source for this poem is the much-debated biblical story of Jesus in the house of Mary and Martha, Luke 10:38–42. Kipling uses it to offer the secular message that people fall into two distinct categories – the workers (sons of Martha) and the non-workers (sons of Mary).

'A Song of Travel' (p. 125). *Morning Post*, 12 March 1908, with article 'The Road to Quebec'; *Songs from Books*. The article is reprinted, without the poem, in *Letters of Travel* (1920). Lines 1–2, Hero and Leander were legendary lovers separated by the Hellespont, which Leander would swim every night, guided by 'the lamp that Hero lit'; line 6, Argo, the ship commanded by Jason in his search for the golden fleece. The poem owes much to Edgar Allan Poe's poem 'To Helen' (1831).

'The Power of the Dog' (p. 126). Closing poem to the story 'Garm – A Hostage', *Actions and Reactions* (1909); *Songs from Books*.

'The Puzzler' (p. 127). Closing poem to the story of the same name, *Actions and Reactions*; expanded for *Songs from Books*. Kipling made less of a contribution to the popular stereotype of the Englishman as strong, silent, thinking slowly but acting decisively, than is often assumed. This, however, is one such contribution. The Celt (lines 1, 19), from Wales to Ireland, from Spain to Scotland. Line 16, *argot*, slang; Remove, an intermediate form or class at public schools.

'The Rabbi's Song' (p. 128). Closing poem to the story 'The House Surgeon', *Actions and Reactions*; *Songs from Books*. The story concerns the exorcism of a house, the haunting being psychological rather than supernatural. The biblical reference given by Kipling is alluded to directly in the final stanza of the poem. It is not clear why it should be a rabbi speaking, though it probably refers to Robert Browning's poem 'Rabbi Ben Ezra' (1864), an optimistic assertion of complete trust in God. Kipling's rabbi qualifies this view by recognizing the power of the mind to turn to and spread the forces of Evil.

'A Charm' (p. 129). Introductory poem to *Rewards and Fairies* (1910); *Songs from Books*. Lines 33–4 were dropped from *Songs from Books* and the *Definitive Edition*, though restored for the *Sussex Edition* of *Rewards and Fairies*. Line 26, Candlemas, 2 February, the feast of the purification of the Virgin Mary; line 27, simples, medicines.

'Cold Iron' (p. 130). Closing poem to the story of the same name, *Rewards and Fairies*; *Songs from Books*. Iron was traditionally supposed to fend off supernatural forces, hence horseshoes nailed to house and stable doors. The precise nature of Kipling's religious beliefs is a matter for conjecture, though this poem is clearly an expression of Christian faith, with the metallic symbols of earthly power and superstition being superseded by the greater redemptive power of the iron nails that held Christ to the cross. Lines 25–8, not exact biblical references, but see Luke 24:30; John 20:27 and 21:12.

'The Looking-Glass' (p. 132). Closing poem to the story 'Gloriana', *Rewards and Fairies*; *Songs from Books*. Line 1, *Harry*, King Henry VIII; line 3, King Philip II of Spain; lines 3–4, Kipling added a note to the *Definitive Edition*: 'A pair of Queen Elizabeth's shoes are still at Brickwall House, Northiam, Sussex'; line 15, Mary Queen of Scots, put to death by Elizabeth; line 22, Robert Dudley, Earl of Leicester, one-time favourite of Elizabeth.

'The Way through the Woods' (p. 133). Opening poem to the story 'Marklake Witches', *Rewards and Fairies*; *Songs from Books*.

'If –' (p. 134). Closing poem to the story 'Brother Square Toes', *Rewards and Fairies*; *Songs from Books*, and subsequently in many different forms. Kipling claimed that the poem was based on the character of Dr L.S. Jameson, leader of the 'Jameson raid' which helped precipitate the Boer War: he also described the poem as made up of 'counsels of perfection most easy to give'. The enormous popularity the poem once enjoyed and the mockery it has provoked have tended to obscure the good sense it contains and the epigrammatic skill of many of its precepts.

'Poor Honest Men' (p. 135). Closing poem to the story 'A Priest in Spite of Himself', *Rewards and Fairies*; *Songs from Books*. The historical setting is dated 1800. A similar subject to 'A Smuggler's Song', though treated quite differently. Line 12, press, to be forcibly enlisted in the navy; line 27, King George III; line 37, Forties and Fifties, the 'roaring' ocean winds of the South Atlantic; line 40, Ushant, an Atlantic island off the French coast.

'Our Fathers of Old' (p. 137). Closing poem to the story 'A Doctor of Medicine', *Rewards and Fairies*; *Songs from Books*. Line 16, the astrological belief that all things on earth are governed by the stars; line 28, blister and bleed, to raise blisters on the skin and to draw blood from the body as ways of curing illnesses; line 35, to signify that the house contained plague victims; lines 41–2, Galen and Hippocrates, ancient Greek physicians and writers on medicine.

'The Declaration of London' (p. 139). *Morning Post*, 29 June 1911; *The Years Between*. In the years prior to the First World War there were many attempts to regulate international shipping and to control the naval arms race between nations. In 1911 the Liberal government put forward a Naval Prize Bill (based on proposals known as 'The Declaration of London', drawn up two years earlier) which would have restricted Britain's ability in time of war to import food and to establish a naval blockade against an enemy. There was widespread opposition to the Bill and it was defeated in the Lords. Kipling's contribution to the campaign was this poem. That the objectors were right to be concerned was proved three years later in the war with Germany. Line 10, the coronation of George V was held on 22 June in Westminster Abbey (line 2). While the event was still being celebrated, with foreign 'guests' (some of them potential 'foes') still in London, Parliament re-assembled on 26 June to debate a policy that if accepted would betray Britain to those same guests/foes.

'The Female of the Species' (p. 140). *Morning Post*, 20 October 1911; *The Years*

Between. Written in response to the militant activity of the Suffragettes, it provoked replies, parodies and objections from feminists, among them Kipling's seventeen-year-old daughter.

'The River's Tale' (p. 142). Introductory poem to *A History of England* (1911) by C.R.L. Fletcher, with poems by Kipling, written 'for all boys and girls who are interested in the story of Great Britain and her Empire'.

'The Roman Centurion's Song' (p. 144). *A History of England*. Kipling's poems and stories about the Roman Empire carry, implicitly, comparisons with the British Empire. Similar feelings to those expressed by the Roman centurion are to be found elsewhere in poems about India, Burma, and South Africa. Line 1, Legate, the governor of a province; cohort, a body of soldiers similar in size to a British battalion; line 2, Portus Itius, a Roman sea-port in France; line 5, Vectis, the Isle of Wight; line 17, Rhodanus, the Rhône; line 18, Nemausus, Nîmes in the south of France; line 19, Arelate, Arles, also in southern France; line 20, Euroclydon, the North East Wind; line 21, the Aurelian Road, running down the Italian coast and home to Rome.

'Dane-Geld' (p. 145). *A History of England*. The *History* explains that King Ethelred's parliament advised him to 'buy off the Danes with hard cash called "Danegold" or "Dane-Geld". The Danes pocketed the silver pennies, laughed, and came back for more.' The historical setting of the poem is given as AD 980–1016, but when the *History* was published in 1911 Kipling would also have had in mind contemporary Britain's increasingly hostile relations with Germany.

'The French Wars' (p. 146). *A History of England*. Kipling's great love of France began when he was a schoolboy and never wavered. Here he sets, against the traditional image of France as Britain's natural enemy, contemporary sea-sick passengers trudging through Customs. Diplomacy prior to the First World War had already established that Britain and France would be allies in any war with Germany. Line 13, Sluys, a naval battle between Britain and France in 1340; line 15, Seventy-fours, the number of guns carried by a battleship; line 16, *chasse-marées*, coastal vessels often used in the Napoleonic wars for smuggling.

'The Glory of the Garden' (p. 147). *A History of England*. The closing poem of the book; a classic Kipling statement that life is service, work, dedication, in whatever capacity. The garden may be grand but it is the gardeners who make it so, not the owners. The image of England as a garden descends from Elizabethan literature, especially Shakespeare: there are also clear biblical allusions to Genesis.

'For All We Have and Are' (p. 148). *The Times*, 2 September 1914; *The Years Between*. Germany declared war on France on 3 August 1914: Britain declared war on Germany the following day. It was a war that Kipling had long expected and he put the blame for it entirely on Germany. Line 4, the word Hun was generally used to describe any barbarous or uncivilized person, after the Asiatic tribes which invaded Europe in the fourth century AD. Only now (though for the same reason) was it applied specifically to the Germans.

'Mine Sweepers' (p. 150). *Daily Telegraph*, 23 November 1915, with article 'The Auxiliaries II'. *The Fringes of the Fleet* (1915); *Sea Warfare* (1916). Mines had long been a familiar part of naval warfare, though they were first extensively deployed in the First World War. The first vessels designed to deal with the problem were adapted fishing trawlers, with wires stretched between two ships which 'swept' or 'trawled' mines to the surface of the water so that they could be destroyed. Line 1, North and South Foreland, headlands on the eastern coast of Kent, used for guarding the Thames estuary; line 5, fairway, the navigable channel leading to the entrance of a harbour; line 7, some of the ships' names in the refrain were real, some invented; line 9, bight, an area of sea between two promontories; line 17, syreens, sirens.

'Tin Fish' (p. 150). *Daily Telegraph*, 27 November 1915, with article 'Submarines II'; *The Fringes of the Fleet*; *Sea Warfare*.

'The Trade' (p. 151). *The Times*, 21 June 1916, with article 'Some Work in the Baltic'; *Tales of 'The Trade'*; *Sea Warfare*. An earlier version of this poem was written for the first number of *The Maidstone Muckrag*, October 1914, a magazine produced by the men of the Eighth Submarine Flotilla of the Royal Navy. 'The Trade' was the term used by the men of the Submarine Service to describe their work: the precise origin of the term is unknown. Lines 1–2, early submarines were classified by letters and numbers: Kipling was writing about E-type submarines; line 5, as they were designed to operate on the surface of the sea as well as underwater they carried guns capable of shooting down Zeppelins; line 7, the range of these particular submarines was not great, and reaching as far as the Baltic was regarded as extremely daring; line 9, prize-courts, able to award part of the proceeds from the sale of captured enemy vessels to the captors; line 18, the Swin, a shoal in the northern approaches to the Thames estuary; line 23, one-eyed, periscope.

'My Boy Jack' (p. 152). *The Times*, 19 October 1916, with the first of four articles 'Destroyers at Jutland'; *Destroyers at Jutland* (1916); *Sea Warfare*. The Battle of Jutland, in the North Sea May/June 1916, was the only major naval engagement between the British and German fleets in the First World War. British losses of ships and men were considerably heavier than those of the Germans, but it was the German fleet that remained in port for the rest of the war, making it at least a tactical British victory.

'The Question' (p. 153). Published as a copyright pamphlet in America, 1916, and as the closing poem of *Sea Warfare*, with the title 'The Neutral'. It was an attempt to stir America to enter the war in support of Britain. The strength of Kipling's feelings can be seen by the tart footnote the poem carries in the *Definitive Edition*: 'Attitude of the United States of America during the first two years, seven months and four days of the Great War.' America declared war on Germany on 6 April 1917 and Kipling wrote a poem, 'The Choice', praising the change of policy and welcoming America into the war.

'Mesopotamia' (p. 154). *Morning Post*, 11 July 1917; *The Years Between*. Written in response to the publication of an official report on the terrible mismanagement of the Mesopotamian campaign, early 1916. The initial purpose of the campaign, which was organized by the Indian government with support from Britain, was to protect oil interests, but it turned into an attempt to capture Baghdad and resulted in the surrender of the British army to Turkey at Kut Al-Amara on 29 April 1916. After the war Mesopotamia (now Iraq) became a British Mandate.

'The Holy War' (p. 155). *Land and Water*, 6 December 1917; *The Years Between*. John Bunyan (1628–88), the son of a tinker and apprenticed to the same trade, fought for the parliamentarians under General Fairfax in the English Civil War. He became a Baptist minister in 1657 and after the Restoration in 1660 he was imprisoned for twelve years; wrote *The Pilgrim's Progress* (1678), and *The Holy War* (1682) in which Kipling sees a complete anticipation of the progress of the First World War. In Bunyan's allegory the town of Mansoul is besieged by the forces of Diabolus but is eventually saved by Emmanuel, the son of the King of Mansoul. The type-names in the poem are from Bunyan or adaptations by Kipling. Line 6, Armageddon, Revelation 16:16, the site of the last great battle before the Day of Judgement; lines 29–30, probably conscientious objectors and pacifists; line 35, Apollyon, the Angel of the Abyss, Revelation 9:9; line 36, Stockholmites, neutrals (i.e. following the example of Sweden); line 42, Bunhill Fields, the Nonconformists' cemetery in the City of London where Bunyan is buried; lines 51–2, Daniel Defoe, another Nonconformist, is usually described as the 'Father of the English novel', but Bunyan's religious allegories showed him the way.

'Jobson's Amen' (p. 157). First two stanzas used as epigraph to an article 'A Return to the East', *Nash's Magazine*, July 1914, but the complete poem at the close of the story 'In the Presence', *A Diversity of Creatures* (1917). The story is based on the actual experiences of four Gurkhas taking on heroic ceremonial duties at King Edward VII's lying-in-state. The poem is an ironic comment on British boastfulness and religiosity, with Jobson's 'Amen' celebrating instead the freer atmosphere (and, as the story demonstrates, the greater endurance) of the East. The reason for using the name Jobson is not clear: there are several possible meanings. *Hobson-Jobson* is the title of the standard dictionary of Anglo-Indian phrases, first published in 1886: it describes religious excitement or enthusiasm, and this could apply here. The endurance demonstrated in the story is also worthy of 'Job'.

'The Fabulists' (p. 158). First published in *A Diversity of Creatures*, misleadingly as the second of two closing poems to the story 'My Son's Wife', though subsequently as the opening poem of the story 'The Vortex'. In the *Definitive Edition* it carries the date 1914–18, to indicate that the tormented thought processes it traces are related directly to the war.

'Justice' (p. 159). *The Times*, 24 October 1918; *The Years Between*. An armistice between the Allies and Germany was finally reached on 11 November 1918. Three weeks before that date Kipling is warning that true 'justice' can be achieved only if a lasting peace is obtained. He was convinced that Germany still had the power and the will to prepare for another war.

'The Hyaenas' (p. 160). *The Years Between*. Line 2, kites, birds of prey. The 'hyaenas' of the poem are the politicians who were dividing up the post-war world and, in the process, betraying the dead.

'En-Dor' (p. 161). *The Years Between*. Kipling's son John died in the Battle of Loos, September 1915: his body was never recovered. While Kipling's wife continued to hope that John might have been taken prisoner, Kipling himself had less hope. Along with many other parents in the same position, the Kiplings received approaches from spiritualists claiming to be able to put them in touch with their dead son. The biblical reference indicates the ancient nature of the experience, while the uncertain date (1914–19–?) added to the poem's title in the *Definitive Edition* suggests, presumably, that the experience is also unending.

'Gethsemane' (p. 163). *The Years Between*. Matthew 26:36–9. Gas was first used by Germany at the second battle of Ypres (April/May 1915), after which gas-masks (line 7) were issued to troops; to ship, to have something ready for use.

'The Craftsman' (p. 163). *The Years Between*. Line 1, The Mermaid Tavern, Bread Street, London, where Elizabethan writers gathered to drink and talk, as Shakespeare and Jonson do here; line 2, Boanerges, Mark 3:17 where the name means Sons of Thunder. Kipling used it several times to refer to someone who is loud, overbearing, or quarrelsome, as Ben Jonson was reputed to be.

'The Benefactors' (p. 164). The opening two stanzas were used as an epigraph to the story 'The Edge of the Evening', *A Diversity of Creatures*; the full poem, *The Years Between*. Lines 5–8, close to views expressed in Robert Browning's 'Fra Lippo Lippi' (1855). The view of life in this poem returns to that expressed by Kipling as early as *Departmental Ditties*, though now sharpened by the experience of the First World War (lines 37–8) and its uncertain aftermath (lines 41–4).

'Natural Theology' (p. 166). *The Years Between*. The title refers to theology based on reasoning from natural observation rather than revelation. Kipling is alluding to Robert Browning's poem 'Caliban upon Setebos; or Natural Theology in the Island' (1864). Like Caliban, the various speakers here justify their beliefs, or lack of belief, in terms of their own narrow views of life. Line 35, the battle of Mons, August 1914, was the opening engagement of the war. The British Expeditionary Force joined up with the French army and both were forced to retreat from the advancing Germans. It was at Mons that an 'Angel' was said to have appeared to inspire British troops.

'Epitaphs of the War' (p. 168). *The Years Between*. Kipling worked for the Imperial War Graves Commission from September 1917 to the end of his life. He made many visits to war cemeteries in Europe, advised on all aspects of the Commission's work, wrote pamphlets and reports, and composed a large number of epitaphs for the memorials to the dead erected throughout the world. It was at Kipling's suggestion that 'Their name liveth for evermore' (Ecclesiasticus, 44) was adopted as the general inscription for all war graves. However, 'Epitaphs of War', as published in *The Years Between* and reprinted here, were works of the imagination, commemorations modelled on *The Greek Anthology*, with, Kipling insisted, 'neither personal nor geographical basis'. In the *Definitive Edition* the Canadian epitaphs are not differentiated, but are simply called 'Two Canadian Memorials': the present wording follows the *Sussex Edition*. Sepoy, Indian soldier serving in the British Army; Halfa, in Mesopotamia; 'The Refined Man', the *Definitive Edition* has 'stepped aside'; 'Native Water-Carrier (M.E.F.)', Mediterranean Expeditionary Force; Tarentum, the Gulf of Taranto, Italy; V.A.D., Voluntary Aid Detachment (nursing service).

'The Gods of the Copybook Headings' (p. 175). *Sunday Pictorial*, 26 October 1919; *Inclusive Edition* (1927). Copybook headings are basic truths or maxims set for a child to copy when learning to write. Kipling places these fundamental truths against the transient values of the market-place. 'Cambrian', 'Feminian', and 'Carboniferous' (lines 17, 21, 25) are not to be taken strictly as geological terms: they indicate areas of post-war discontent. Line 35, II Peter 2:22; line 36, wabbling, wobbling.

'The Clerks and the Bells' (p. 178). *Nash's Magazine*, February 1920; *Inclusive Edition* (1927). In the years following the war Kipling became very interested in university education. He wrote several poems on the subject, though none stranger than this poem which presents a stereotypical image of a medieval Oxford devoted to prayer and study as well as to luxury and comfort, an image constantly challenged by the experiences of trench warfare which the students have brought back with them to university.

'Lollius' (p. 180). *Q. Horati Flacci Carminum Liber Quintus* (1920) by Kipling and Charles Graves. Kipling's interest in the poetry of Horace dated from his schooldays, though it is mainly in his later work that the influence becomes apparent. He wrote several 'imitations' of Horace, and contributed 'Lollius' to this book which, purporting to be the non-existent Fifth Book of Horace's Odes, was a gentle scholarly joke. The poem probably had some personal significance for Kipling: unlike Lollius (who was a wealthy, successful friend of Horace's), Kipling steadfastly refused to accept any of the public honours and awards offered him by successive British governments. Line 3, nard, aromatic oil.

'London Stone' (p. 181). *The Times*, 10 November 1923. *Inclusive Edition* 1927. Written to commemorate Armistice Day, 11 November.

'Doctors' (p. 182). Dated 1923 in the *Definitive Edition*, where it was first published.

'Chartres Windows' (p. 182). *Daily Telegraph*, 15 April 1925; *Inclusive Edition* (1927). Written to accompany an article 'Stained Glass in Western France' by Perceval Landon, a close friend of Kipling's. Line 5, purfled, decorated with; line 7, grozed, trimmed.

'The Changelings' (p. 183). Opening poem to the story 'Sea Constables', *Debits and Credits* (1926). R.N.V.R., Royal Naval Volunteer Reserve. Lines 1–2, before the sinking of passenger liners by German U-boats; line 18, pied, camouflaged; lines 19–20, Psalms 107:26.

'Gipsy Vans' (p. 184). Opening poem to the story 'A Madonna of the Trenches', *Debits and Credits*. Line 11, Gorgio, the Romany term for a non-gipsy; line 12, Romany, a gipsy and the gipsy language; line 35, ryes, Romany for gentlemen.

'A Legend of Truth' (p. 185). Opening poem to the story 'A Friend of the Family', *Debits and Credits*. The conflict between Truth (or Fact) and Fiction is based on Aristotle's claim in the *Poetics* that poetry is more philosophical than history because it deals with universal rather than particular truths. Line 6, Pilate's question, to Jesus, 'What is truth?' John 18:37-8; lines 7-8, Galileo, forced by the Church to renounce his great astronomical discoveries.

'We and They' (p. 187). Closing poem to the story 'A Friend of the Family', *Debits and Credits*.

'Untimely' (p. 188). Opening poem to the story 'The Eye of Allah', *Debits and Credits*. The story deals with the early invention of a microscope which is destroyed by the Church out of fear that it will challenge Christian faith, even though its inventor claims it will help cure illness and thus glorify the Church. Kipling's point is that advanced knowledge is often stifled by fear and conformity until its 'timely' moment for recognition arrives. Line 12, to Earth, on earth prior to *Sussex*.

'A Rector's Memory' (p. 189). *St Andrews* (1926), containing this poem; 'A Memory' by Walter de la Mare; and sketches by Malcolm Patterson, all contributed to help raise money for a student welfare scheme. Not collected until *Definitive Edition*. Kipling was Rector of the University of St Andrews, which is situated on the Fife coast facing the North Sea (lines 15-18), from 1922 to 1925.

'Memories' (p. 190). *The Daily Telegraph*, 3 November 1930; *Inclusive Edition* (1933). Kipling's anger was aroused at a statement issued by Ramsay MacDonald's second Labour government that foreign officials need not feel obliged to observe Armistice Day unless they wished to. Line 3, Mark 9:44; line 12, to appease Germany.

'Gertrude's Prayer' (p. 191). The closing poem to the story 'Dayspring Mishandled', *Limits and Renewals* (1932), where it carries an explanatory note 'Modernized from the "Chaucer" of Manallace'. In the story Manallace forges a fragment of Chaucer in order to fool, and by doing so have revenge on, a distinguished literary scholar: initially the revenge is successful but rebounds upon Manallace. Line 6, Dayspring, day-break; line 9, girt, girth; line 10, wried, twisted; line 11, gall, a sore or blister; wen, a wart or tumour; line 17, Jesu-Moder, Mother of Jesus.

'Four-Feet' (p. 191). Closing poem to the story 'The Woman in his Life', *Limits and Renewals*.

'The Disciple' (p. 192). Closing poem to the story 'The Church that was at Antioch', *Limits and Renewals*. Lines 35-6, Carpenter (Christ); Cameleer (Mohammed); Maya's dreaming son (Buddha).

'The Threshold' (p. 193). Closing poem to the story 'Unprofessional', *Limits and Renewals*. The extremely complex story is about a group of modern medical researchers who discover that astrology has a key role to play in their treatment of a patient suffering from cancer: the poem pursues this theme of 'professional' and 'unprofessional' knowledge. Ionia, c. 1000 BC, situated on the coast of Asia Minor (now Turkey), initiated the developments that came to typify ancient Greek civilization. The philosophers of Ionia (usually referred to as 'pre-Socratic') sought to trace the laws of the universe to one physical source ('Matter', line 29), thus dispelling earlier concepts of knowledge founded on primitive superstition. The Ionians were in turn superseded, and their sense of the wholeness or oneness of human experience rejected, by a resurgence of superstition and the fragmentation of modern knowledge.

'The Expert' (p. 195). Closing poem to the story 'Beauty Spots', *Limits and Renewals*. The story is humorous in tone, the poem serious. The main theme of the poem – that young men trained in violence in wartime are capable of applying their violent skills to the very different circumstances of civilian life – has become a major concern in studies of the after-effects of more recent wars. Line 17, No-Man's Land, the deserted, devastated areas of land between the trenches of conflicting armies.

'The Storm Cone' (p. 196). *Morning Post*, 23 May 1932; *Inclusive Edition* (1933). Throughout the 1920s and early 1930s Kipling kept a close watch on the rehabilitation of post-war Germany and the rise of Nazism. This poem is one of several public pronouncements that there can no longer be any doubt about Germany's expansionist and militaristic intentions. Storm cones, black canvas cones hoisted at coastguard stations to warn of gales approaching. Line 17, They fall and whelm, the waves sink and rise again, threatening to engulf the ship, in this instance, Britain, the Ship of State.

'The Bonfires' (p. 197). *Morning Post*, 13 November 1933, as 'Bonfires on the Ice'; *Definitive Edition*. Published to coincide with two significant events – Armistice Sunday (the previous day) and the announcement of the results of a referendum in Germany which gave overwhelming support to Hitler. Line 15, Bobtailed Flush, a poker hand consisting of four cards of the same suit, one short of a 'full' flush; line 18, Demos, the people; line 19, the Fenris Wolf, Fenrir or Fenrisulfr, savage wolf of Norse mythology and a symbol of evil; line 22, Cockatrice, a legendary serpent or basilisk, able to kill by a glance.

'The Appeal' (p. 198). *Definitive Edition*.

Index of Titles

Index of First Lines

Visit Penguin on the Internet
and browse at your leisure

- preview sample extracts of our forthcoming books
- read about your favourite authors
- investigate over 10,000 titles
- enter one of our literary quizzes
- win some fantastic prizes in our competitions
- e-mail us with your comments and book reviews
- instantly order any Penguin book

and masses more!

'To be recommended without reservation ... a rich and rewarding on-line experience' – Internet Magazine

www.penguin.co.uk

READ MORE IN PENGUIN

In every corner of the world, on every subject under the sun, Penguin represents quality and variety – the very best in publishing today.

For complete information about books available from Penguin – including Puffins, Penguin Classics and Arkana – and how to order them, write to us at the appropriate address below. Please note that for copyright reasons the selection of books varies from country to country.

In the United Kingdom: Please write to *Dept. EP, Penguin Books Ltd, Bath Road, Harmondsworth, West Drayton, Middlesex UB7 ODA*

In the United States: Please write to *Consumer Sales, Penguin USA, P.O. Box 999, Dept. 17109, Bergenfield, New Jersey 07621-0120*. VISA and MasterCard holders call 1-800-253-6476 to order Penguin titles

In Canada: Please write to *Penguin Books Canada Ltd, 10 Alcorn Avenue, Suite 300, Toronto, Ontario M4V 3B2*

In Australia: Please write to *Penguin Books Australia Ltd, P.O. Box 257, Ringwood, Victoria 3134*

In New Zealand: Please write to *Penguin Books (NZ) Ltd, Private Bag 102902, North Shore Mail Centre, Auckland 10*

In India: Please write to *Penguin Books India Pvt Ltd, 706 Eros Apartments, 56 Nehru Place, New Delhi 110 019*

In the Netherlands: Please write to *Penguin Books Netherlands bv, Postbus 3507, NL-1001 AH Amsterdam*

In Germany: Please write to *Penguin Books Deutschland GmbH, Metzlerstrasse 26, 60594 Frankfurt am Main*

In Spain: Please write to *Penguin Books S. A., Bravo Murillo 19, 1° B, 28015 Madrid*

In Italy: Please write to *Penguin Italia s.r.l., Via Felice Casati 20, I–20124 Milano*

In France: Please write to *Penguin France S. A., 17 rue Lejeune, F–31000 Toulouse*

In Japan: Please write to *Penguin Books Japan, Ishikiribashi Building, 2–5–4, Suido, Bunkyo-ku, Tokyo 112*

In South Africa: Please write to *Longman Penguin Southern Africa (Pty) Ltd, Private Bag X08, Bertsham 2013*

READ MORE IN PENGUIN

A SELECTION OF POETRY

American Verse
British Poetry since 1945
Caribbean Verse in English
Chinese Love Poetry
A Choice of Comic and Curious Verse
Contemporary American Poetry
Contemporary British Poetry
Contemporary Irish Poetry
English Poetry 1918–60
English Romantic Verse
English Verse
First World War Poetry
German Verse
Greek Verse
Homosexual Verse
Imagist Poetry
Irish Verse
Japanese Verse
The Metaphysical Poets
Modern African Poetry
New Poetry
Poetry of the Thirties
Scottish Verse
Surrealist Poetry in English
Spanish Verse
Victorian Verse
Women Poets
Zen Poetry

READ MORE IN PENGUIN

POETRY LIBRARY

Blake	Selected by W. H. Stevenson
Browning	Selected by Daniel Karlin
Burns	Selected by Angus Calder and William Donnelly
Byron	Selected by A. S. B. Glover
Clare	Selected by Geoffrey Summerfield
Coleridge	Selected by Richard Holmes
Donne	Selected by John Hayward
Dryden	Selected by Douglas Grant
Hardy	Selected by David Wright
Housman	Introduced by John Sparrow
Keats	Selected by John Barnard
Kipling	Selected by Craig Raine
Lawrence	Selected by Keith Sagar
Milton	Selected by Laurence D. Lerner
Pope	Selected by Douglas Grant
Rubáiyát of Omar Khayyám	Translated by Edward FitzGerald
Shelley	Selected by Isabel Quigly
Tennyson	Selected by W. E. Williams
Wordsworth	Selected by Nicholas Roe
Yeats	Selected by Timothy Webb

READ MORE IN PENGUIN

RUDYARD KIPLING

'The most complete man of genius I have ever known' – Henry James

The Light That Failed
A Diversity of Creatures
The Day's Work
Debits and Credits
Wee Willie Winkie
Just So Stories
Traffics and Discoveries
Short Stories
  Volumes I and II
Selected Stories
Kim

The Jungle Books
Life's Handicap
Limits and Renewals
Something of Myself
Plain Tales from the Hills
Puck of Pook's Hill
Rewards and Fairies
Selected Poems
Soldiers Three *and* **In Black**
  and White

'For my own part I worshipped Kipling at thirteen, loathed him at seventeen, enjoyed him at twenty, despised him at twenty-five, and now again rather admire him. The one thing that was never possible, if one had read him at all, was to forget him' – George Orwell